gluten-free
vegan

COMFORT FOOD

125

simple and satisfying recipes,

from "mac n' cheese" to chocolate cupcakes

SUSAN O'BRIEN

Da Capo
LIFE
LONG

A MEMBER OF THE PERSEUS BOOKS GROUP

Copyright © 2012 by Susan O'Brien

Photos by Lara Ferroni

All rights reserved. No part of this publication may be reproduced, stored in a retrieval system, or transmitted, in any form or by any means, electronic, mechanical, photocopying, recording, or otherwise, without the prior written permission of the publisher. Printed in the United States of America. For information, address Da Capo Press, 44 Farnsworth Street, 3rd Floor, Boston, MA 02210.

Editorial production by Lori Hobkirk the Book Factory
Designed in Caslon by Cynthia Young at Sagecraft

Cataloging-in-Publication data for this book is available from the Library of Congress.

First Da Capo Press edition 2012

ISBN: 978-0-7382-1490-0

ISBN: 978-0-7382-1550-1 (e-book)

Published by Da Capo Press
A Member of the Perseus Books Group
www.dacapopress.com

Note: The information in this book is true and complete to the best of our knowledge. This book is intended only as an informative guide for those wishing to know more about health issues. In no way is this book intended to replace, countermand, or conflict with the advice given to you by your own physician. The ultimate decision concerning care should be made between you and your doctor. We strongly recommend you follow his or her advice. Information in this book is general and is offered with no guarantees on the part of the authors or Da Capo Press. The authors and publisher disclaim all liability in connection with the use of this book. The names and identifying details of people associated with events described in this book have been changed. Any similarity to actual persons is coincidental.

Da Capo Press books are available at special discounts for bulk purchases in the U.S. by corporations, institutions, and other organizations. For more information, please contact the Special Markets Department at the Perseus Books Group, 2300 Chestnut Street, Suite 200, Philadelphia, PA, 19103, or call (800) 810-4145, ext. 5000, or e-mail special.markets@perseusbooks.com.

10 9 8 7 6 5 4 3 2 1

gluten-free
vegan
COMFORT FOOD

Dedicated to Carol Dudley
In memory of Richard Berthiaume

contents

7 Family Classics 125

8 Ethnic Favorites 147

9 Delightful Desserts 165

foreword

Gluten-free, vegan, AND comfort food—one might think that these are mutually exclusive! Well, wait until you begin trying some of these recipes.

As a nurse and nutrition consultant, I could have used a cookbook like this all the years I have been counseling patients to remove gluten and dairy—the hidden sources of food intolerance and health problems—from their diets. It would have made my life much easier. In the past few years, there has been a burgeoning amount of gluten-free selections (foods that are free of the protein found in wheat, rye, and barley) on menus and in supermarkets. However, these foods do not taste like Susan O'Brien's gluten-free foods, especially as her recipes use healthier sweeteners like maple syrup.

As the years go by, I have really begun to understand how important it is for my patients to still be able to indulge in comfort foods. Let's face it, no one wants to give up lasagna or chocolate! Yet all the recipes (and the packaged foods we find in grocery stores) for our favorite foods often contain gluten and/or dairy. I'll admit, I found it hard to imagine Sue coming up with 125 delicious recipes that fit the bill.

Then I tried her recipes—they were beyond what I thought gluten-free, vegan foods could taste like! I also was very pleased to see some new ingredients offered in her book. Chia seeds (high in healthy omega-3 fats), coconut oil, and coconut milk are foods that many of us hadn't cooked with much before. In fact, many people think that coconut is unhealthy. Nothing could be further from the truth! Coconut has many benefits, which Sue discusses in this book's Introduction. Read the Introduction carefully because you will learn a lot about the health benefits of foods that you may not have been aware of.

People who follow a traditional vegetarian diet often eat quite a lot of foods containing gluten and dairy. But those who avoid dairy, gluten, and animal products often notice that they feel better in general, that their energy is higher, and that they are experiencing fewer digestive problems and joint aches.

So, you are not 100 percent vegan or vegetarian? Or you don't usually avoid dairy, gluten, or eggs? This matters not—you'll still love these recipes. It's healthy to rotate your diet so that you don't eat the same foods every day; in fact, research suggests that it is healthy to eat a vegetarian/meatless meal several times a week or more. These recipes make this so easy to do.

It's time to start your journey to better health, while enjoying yourself along the way. Thank you, Sue!

Barb Schlitz, RN, MS
Nutrition Consultant

introduction

Many of my readers wrote to me and asked me to develop a sequel to *The Gluten-Free Vegan*. I heard over and over again how many of you longed for gluten-free, vegan recipes for your favorite foods. So I responded resolutely . . . yes! This cookbook contains many easy-to-make comfort foods that you will love, all free of gluten, dairy, eggs, and animal products.

You are not going to believe the fun you will have with the delicious recipes in this cookbook! From the black bean burgers to the peanut butter and chocolate chip–rice cereal treats, this cookbook is full of mouthwatering recipes. Some of my favorites include Roasted Beet Risotto; Vegetable Potpie; Chocolate, Zucchini, and Apple Bread; Pumpkin Waffles; Best Banana and Chocolate Chip Cookies; and . . . I could go on and on. The recipes are made with fresh herbs and spices and will delight even the most finicky person in your house. No matter where you live, or what time of year it is, you will be able to enjoy wholesome, delicious foods!

We all crave certain foods. At times, we want a meal or dessert that is quick and easy to fix and at other times, we want something that nourishes us. These 125 recipes will satisfy your desire for feel-good foods and at the same time, they will support your wellness. Some of the recipes are super-easy to make, such as the Layered Polenta or the Mac and Cheese. Others take a bit more time, but are worth the wait!

With *Gluten-Free Vegan Comfort Food*, I have endeavored to develop a cookbook that fulfills your culinary and nutritional needs. Besides requests for new recipes, many of you have also asked me to develop recipes free of soy, or to eliminate agave cactus nectar as my primary sweetener because of concerns about how it is processed. Some of you have asked that I use only ingredients that are affordable and available at your everyday market.

I have reduced the amount of agave I use in the recipes, integrated organic maple syrup, and explored new sugar alternatives, such as coconut palm sugar. Yes, coconut palm sugar is a bit more expensive, but if you buy it online in bulk it significantly reduces the cost. (Using it in combination with maple syrup also enables you to use less).

I have reduced the number of recipes made with soy and branched out into the world of chia seeds! I love these seeds as they can be used in place of an egg in a recipe, as a thickener for sauces, or as a source of protein in smoothies or soups.

I know you must be wondering if the chia seeds I am referring to are the same Chia Pet seeds that many of us watered as kids and watched sprout "hair" on clay rabbits or dogs and the answer is, Yes, they are the same seeds! The nutritional value in these seeds will knock your socks off. I'll tell you more about them later in the book, in the section on ingredients.

I hope this cookbook will inspire you to be creative. I have always said that my recipes are a "starting place" for you. My testers provided helpful input that I used to make these recipes even better, but there are endless ways to alter dishes, add to them, or use what you have available in your kitchen. Please do not feel like you must have all of the same veggies in a recipe. If you are missing carrots, use broccoli. If you don't have mushrooms, leave them out. Use what you have and what you love—be creative and explore new options that you haven't previously considered. That said, please be careful to read the whole ingredient list before you begin a specific recipe. Several of the recipes include tree nuts or peanuts and some of you may have nut allergies. I highly recommend a read-through so you don't get halfway into a recipe to find out that it has an ingredient that will not be good for your personal health, or that you don't have in the house. It's quite annoying to have to run to the market for a single ingredient!

This book was created with love and pure intention. If you put that into every recipe you make, you will not only enjoy each meal you prepare, but you will derive energy from the foods that will support your physical, emotional, and spiritual well-being.

My very best wishes to you all,

Susan O'Brien

about the ingredients

What's New?

With *Gluten-Free Vegan Comfort Food*, I have added some new ingredients to my recipes, and I have also changed some of the ingredients I have used in previous cookbooks. Let's take a look at what's new in this cookbook.

Tempeh is a food I haven't included in previous cookbooks. It is a great whole food choice if you are not allergic or sensitive to soy.

Tempeh originated in Indonesia and is available all over the world in grocery stores or health food stores. It is made from soybeans that have been dehulled, mixed with a tempeh starter, formed into a cake, and then cooked. Some companies that make tempeh have expanded from the original version, making it with veggies, herbs, spices, and additional grains. It is a fiber-rich food that is a great source of protein, and it has no cholesterol. It is also a good source of calcium, vitamin B, and iron. Be sure to read the ingredient list before you purchase tempeh as some varieties may contain soy sauce that is made with wheat.

Check out the Tempeh Tacos on page 159 or Barbara's Special Marinated Tempeh recipe on page 127. Tempeh is so versatile, you can use it in stir-fries, salads, and a host of other ways.

Chia seeds: I mentioned chia seeds briefly in the Introduction. I am so glad these seeds came into my life! They are such a great source of fiber (3 grams in 1 tablespoon), are incredibly high in omega-3 fatty acids, and they are an excellent substitution for eggs in baked goods! (I use 1 teaspoon mixed with 2 tablespoons water and let it sit for about 5 to 10 minutes). You may be surprised to see them show up in recipes such as Meatless Meatballs (see page 139), but they really hold these meatballs together well and add a lovely light crunch.

Amaranth can be purchased as a flour, seed, or puffed cereal. I like the seed, as it can be used in place of rice or quinoa, and it packs a punch when it comes to its high calcium content. Amaranth is great as a breakfast grain; I eat it almost every morning. An easy recipe is to take 2½ cups of water and bring to a boil. Add 1 cup of amaranth and lower the heat to medium. Cover and let it cook for 15 to 20 minutes, or until thick. Turn off the heat and dish up. I add cinnamon, chopped apples, chopped Medjool dates and/or fresh blueberries, and milk to my cereal. It really fuels your morning!

Organic coconut palm sugar, Sweet Tree, sold by Big Tree Farms, is a new sweetener I recently began using in my recipes with great success. It has been labeled the "most sustainable sweetener" by the Food and Agriculture Organization of the United Nations. I have elected to use this sugar in some of the recipes as I love the texture, the mild sweetness it provides, and the exotic color it adds to recipes. Again, used in moderation—if you do not have a medical condition that prevents you from consuming sugar—it is a good alternative to cane sugar and tastes far better!

Coconut milk (not the canned variety, the boxed variety): I have a sensitivity to both soy and hemp milks, so I was very happy when So Delicious coconut milk hit the market. I love it. Even the creamer that you can use in your morning coffee tastes good, but I have found a way to use the creamer in scones too! This milk comes in French vanilla, unsweetened, and regular flavors. If you don't like this milk, the options to replace it in my recipes would be a soy, hemp, or hazelnut milk. You can experiment with some nut milks, like the Creamy Cashew Milk recipe (page 206), but be careful as coconut milk has a thicker consistency than rice milk and some nut milks too.

Full-fat coconut milk (the canned variety): I have used canned coconut milk for ages. Its value in curries and rice puddings is priceless, but I must admit that I have changed my opinion on using lite over regular coconut milk—the lite version is just watered down.

While researchers do not entirely agree yet on the health benefits of coconut, they do agree that 50 percent of the fatty acids in coconut fat are lauric acid, a medium chain fatty acid naturally found in mother's milk. The lauric acid is formed into monolaurin in the human body. Monolaurin is proposed to have antibacterial, antiviral, and antifungal properties.

Virgin coconut oil: This oil really got a bad rap in the past, but it is not unhealthy as it was once thought to be. Organic virgin coconut oil is not chemically treated and does not contain trans fats; it's not the partially hydrogenated coconut oil that researchers conducted their studies on many years ago.

One of the things I like about virgin coconut oil is that it is solid at room temperature and it holds up very well in baked items such as muffins, cakes, scones, and cookies. It has a very light flavor, so it does not overpower the taste of other ingredients.

About the Gluten-Free Diet

Gluten-free (GF) diets are more common now than ever before. Some individuals go on a gluten-free diet because they have a sensitivity or intolerance to gluten, a protein found in wheat, barley, rye, and foods containing these grains. Gluten sensitivity is a systemic condition that manifests in various ways in the body. Some people experience "foggy" brain, bloating, headaches, fatigue, or other symptoms. Others have celiac disease, an autoimmune condition that causes damage to the small intestine and interferes with the absorption of nutrients in food. Those who have this disease must completely avoid all foods and products that contain the gluten protein. According to the National Institutes of Health (NIH), more than two million people in the United States have celiac disease. That is a staggering number. For these folks, avoiding gluten is very important, as they can have terrible reactions or symptoms if they even accidentally consume the protein.

For others, going on a gluten-free diet is a personal choice. Many people want to experiment with different foods, or they may feel better when they avoid products containing gluten. Thanks to all of the gluten-free options available everywhere now, there are wonderful gluten-free restaurants, bakeries, cookbooks, and markets popping up everywhere. Gluten-free never tasted as good as it does now!

Foods to Avoid
on a Gluten-Free Diet

- ✓ Wheat
- ✓ Durum
- ✓ Faro
- ✓ Graham
- ✓ Semolina
- ✓ Rye
- ✓ Spelt
- ✓ Barley
- ✓ Kamut
- ✓ Triticale
- ✓ Baked goods and cereals containing any of the above grains mentioned
- ✓ Beer (except GF beer)
- ✓ Bread
- ✓ Bread Crumbs
- ✓ Cake mixes
- ✓ Crackers, pretzels, and many other "snack" foods)

- ✓ Croutons
- ✓ Gravies, unless you make it yourself with arrowroot or rice flour
- ✓ Soy sauce and teriyaki sauce unless labeled wheat-free
- ✓ Soup bases (unless specified gluten-free)
- ✓ Pastas (except rice, corn, quinoa)
- ✓ Marinades
- ✓ Textured vegetable protein (TVP)
- ✓ Dressings (unless labeled gluten-free)
- ✓ Food starch
- ✓ Communion wafers
- ✓ Some medications and herbal supplements

About the Vegan Diet

A vegan diet is one that excludes all animal products, such as meats, dairy, and eggs. People who choose a vegan diet may do so because they do not want to kill animals for food. They may choose a vegan diet because of health reasons. Those with heart disease, cancer, those who are overweight, and people who wish to improve their health often choose a vegan diet because plant-based diets are good for you! Look at former president Bill Clinton as an example. He had a heart attack a few years ago and he could have died. He is now a vegetarian, and he says he is feeling better than he has for years. If you read Colin Campbell's book, *The China Study*, you will see that eating a plant-based diet will significantly reduce your chances for cancer. Good reason to give a vegan lifestyle a try!

If you have allergies to eggs or dairy products, you may choose a vegan diet. There are so many wonderful substitutions for eggs and dairy products now available (I love chia seeds mixed with water as an egg replacer) that those with allergies can enjoy foods like never before!

The important thing to remember when choosing a vegan diet is to incorporate protein into your diet. There are many foods that will incorporate protein in a vegan diet, including nuts, grains, legumes, tofu, and vegetables, just to name a few.

Dairy/Casein Foods to Avoid

✓ All bovine milk and milk products
✓ Artificial flavorings
✓ Semisweet chocolate
✓ Chocolate chips (except GF vegan varieties)
✓ White or milk chocolate
✓ Creamed soups
✓ Store-bought puddings and custard

The Gluten-Free Vegan Pantry: Recommended Foods to Stock

Here are many of the items I keep in stock in my pantry. I am sure there are some items that you stock that I don't, so please use this only as a guide.

I choose organic whenever possible, especially with corn or soy products. The organic label is a guarantee that no genetically modified organism (GMO) has been incorporated. If not organic, then you can be sure that the soy or corn product contains GMO corn or soy. I highly recommend you avoid any foods that are genetically modified.

Flours

- Bob's Red Mill All Purpose GF Flour
- Sorghum flour
- Brown rice flour
- Coconut flour
- Quinoa flour
- Millet flour
- Chickpea flour (garbanzo bean)
- Potato flour
- Amaranth flour
- Tapioca flour
- Almond flour
- Buckwheat flour
- Arrowroot flour
- Teff flour

Other Dry Ingredients

- Cornmeal
- Chia seeds
- Flaxseed or flaxmeal
- Almond meal
- Gluten-free oats
- Baking yeast
- Nutritional yeast
- Egg replacer, such as Bob's Red Mill's or Ener-G Foods egg replacer
- Cocoa powder
- Guar gum or xanthum gum

Sweeteners

- Organic maple syrup
- Organic brown rice syrup
- Sorghum syrup
- Organic agave cactus nectar
- Mystic Lake Dairy fruit sweetener
- Stevia
- Organic coconut palm sugar
- Organic cane sugar
- Pure fruit jams
- Applesauce
- Molasses
- Enjoy Life Foods chocolate chips (vegan)

Oils and Other Fats

- Coconut oil, virgin and organic
- Olive oil, cold-pressed and extra virgin
- Organic canola oil (organic is a MUST as it will definitely be GMO if not organic)
- Grapeseed oil, expeller- or cold-pressed
- Spectrum palm shortening
- Earth Balance Natural Buttery Spread
- Spectrum vegan margarine

Pantry Staples

- Brown rice
- Red rice
- Arborio rice
- Wild rice
- Black rice
- Lentils
- Mung beans
- Soybeans
- Kidney, pinto, black, and cannellini beans
- Dried peas and seeds
- Nuts (walnuts, cashews, Brazil nuts, almonds, pecans, macadamia) and seeds (pumpkin, sunflower, sesame, and, of course, pine nuts)
- Raisins, Medjool dates, dried cherries

- Balsamic vinegar, *Bragg* apple cider vinegar, brown rice vinegar
- Tamari (lower-sodium soy sauce), wheat-free (it must state that it is wheat-free, otherwise it is not gluten-free)
- Organic vegetable broth
- Vanilla
- Kosher and sea salts
- Peppercorns
- Fresh and dried herbs
- Spices
- Candied ginger
- Red and white wine

Flours and Starches

For those of you who have celiac disease, or have allergies or sensitivities to gluten, you must seek wheat flour alternatives. The good news is that today there are so many wonderful alternatives available it is not hard to eat well and find the foods satisfying!

Almost every market now stocks some gluten-free flours. If your local market doesn't, I would ask the manager to stock the most common substitutes, as many, many people are now gluten-free, and it is easy for supermarkets to find suppliers. If you live in a big city, the options are endless, as the big health food chains like Whole Foods, Mother's, and others all have dedicated sections for gluten-free products. But, if you don't live in a city, check out your local health food store. It is also possible in today's world to order whatever you need online. If you buy directly from a mill, such as Bob's Red Mill, you may be able to get a better price. Also, there are many gluten-free online stores now that provide excellent prices.

I store my flours in the refrigerator after I open them, but you can also store them in your freezer if you prefer.

Coconut flour: I love cooking with coconut flour. It has a wonderfully light flavor that "softens" the flavor in baked goods. Coconut flour is not cheap, so it is best to buy it in bulk if you can. (Bob's Red Mill sells many GF flours in bulk.) I use it sparingly and keep it in the refrigerator once I have opened it. It provides a good source of calcium and protein, and it is high in fiber. When adding coconut flour to a recipe, do not add too much as it is denser than other GF flours. If I am using it in baked goods, I don't use more than 20 to 25 percent of the total flour for the recipe.

Sorghum flour: This is my all-time favorite flour. It mimics closely the texture of wheat flour, so it holds up well in baked goods. I like to use it in combination with other flours, such as organic brown rice, coconut, millet, quinoa, and bean flours. Sorghum is a staple in India and Africa, and it is very high in fiber. I use it often, as it seems to provide "substance" to baked goods in a way that ensures the finished product does not crumble or fall apart.

Millet flour: This flour originated in China about 5,000 years ago. It is one of the earliest grains used and is a great source of protein, fiber, and amino acids. I love to use this flour in breads, as it has a sweet, light flavor that doesn't overpower the taste of the bread. Try out the Millet Bread recipe on page 101. This bread is great for sandwiches, the Bruschetta recipe found on page 53, as well as the French Toast (page 38). One quarter cup of millet flour provides 3 grams of protein and 2.5 grams of fiber. It has no cholesterol and only 1 gram of total fat, per quarter cup, although none from trans fats or saturated fats.

Teff flour: This grain originated from Ethiopia, and it packs a huge punch of both iron and calcium. It has a rather strong flavor and is best combined with other lighter flours, such as brown rice, potato, or tapioca flour. Used in cookies, muffins, and scones, teff adds protein, texture, and tons of flavor.

Brown rice flour and white rice flour: White rice flour is used occasionally in this book as it adds lightness to recipes—it certainly does help to lighten a loaf of bread!—but in general I try to stay away from the white products as they don't have a lot of nutritional value.

Brown rice flour contains more nutrients than white rice flour and is considered a whole food. It is rated "medium" on the glycemic index (GI) and is full of nutrients such as magnesium, iron, B1 and B3, and some fatty acids, and it is also a good source of fiber. I use this flour alone, and I often use it in combination with sorghum flour, as the combination works well and reduces the cost of using only sorghum flour in a recipe.

Buckwheat flour: So many people are surprised to find out that buckwheat flour is not related to wheat. It is a fruit seed that is related to rhubarb and sorrel. Buckwheat provides B1, B2, magnesium, phosphate, potassium, and more iron than cereal grains. It is also very high in the amino acid lysine, and it contains rutin, which is a flavonoid known to help to reduce cholesterol and lower blood pressure. I use buckwheat flour primarily in my pancake and waffle recipes, but you can certainly add it to other baked goods as well. If you are interested in the health benefits of buckwheat, I recommend you try buckwheat groats. They are available in health food stores and can be used alone as a hot breakfast dish or served as a side dish to a main course.

Quinoa flour: Quinoa (pronounced "keen-wa") has gained much favor over the past few years, and I am sure happy about that. This grain is amazing, not just as flour, but the grain itself can be used in a variety of ways! Both the grain and the flour are high in protein, and they are considered whole foods since they contain all twenty amino acids, including ten "essential amino acids." Quinoa also provides vitamins A, C, D, B1, B2, and E, as well as several minerals and other vitamins. The only downside of this flour is the cost, but if you buy it in bulk, it is much more economical. It blends very nicely with other flours and adds a light, delicate taste.

Garbanzo bean and other legume flours: Garbanzo flour is derived from chickpeas, which are in the legume family. Garbanzo flour is high in protein and low in fat. Chickpeas are also high in folate, phosphorus, and fiber. This flour is great in corn breads, cookies, and bars, and is commonly used in Indian cuisine as well as Asian. Lentil flour and chickpea flours add a creamy texture to the more grainy flours such as rice. I like to combine them into recipes to even out the texture.

Almond flour or almond meal: These two ingredients are made of blanched almonds that have been finely ground. The difference between the flour and the meal is that the meal includes the outer shell of the almond. Almond flour and meal are great sources of protein, vitamin E, and magnesium, and they are high in fiber. They provide a delightfully rich buttery taste to breads, cookies, and biscotti (try the Chocolate–Dried Cherry Biscotti found on page 172).

Potato flour and potato starch: These two are definitely NOT the same! Please check your recipe before venturing out to the market, as the results will not be the same if you pick up the wrong ingredient.

Potato flour is made from potatoes, skin and all. It is a heavy flour, with a distinct potato flavor. It is never used alone in a recipe, as it is way too dense, so it must be combined with a lighter flour so it will not become gummy.

Potato starch, on the other hand, comes from the potato, but the skin is removed and the product is made into a slurry that is then dehydrated, removing the potato flavor, leaving it bland and very starchy. It can make quite a mess in your kitchen, due to its cornstarch-like texture. It is also low in fiber and nutrients, so its purpose is truly to "lighten" recipes. For instance, in bread it can really help to make the finished product less dense.

Tapioca flour: This flour is also referred to as tapioca starch. It originates from Cuba, Puerto Rico, and many South American countries. It is derived from the root of the plant species *Manihot esculenta*, and it is now cultivated all over the world. It doesn't really have much nutritional value—zero protein—but it is commonly used as a thickener. I use it to lighten up recipes, such as in breads, muffins, and biscuits; it has a light but sweet flavor.

Soy flour: I have not used this flour in this book, as I try to avoid soy as much as possible, due to the fact that it is a common allergen and many soy products are genetically modified. Soy flour is high in protein, high in isoflavones, and it is considered a whole food. It should be stored in the refrigerator. It is best to use soy flour in combination with other flours, as its flavor by itself can overpower a recipe. I have used it together with rice and or sorghum flours. You can combine it with many flours if you wish to experiment with it. If not organic, it is likely to be GMO, so organic soy is preferred.

Arrowroot or cornstarch: These starches are used as thickeners in recipes. Arrowroot comes from a plant that is harvested, dried, and then ground into a powdery substance. Unlike cornstarch, it does not need to be mixed with water before adding to your recipe.

I prefer arrowroot to cornstarch, so you won't see cornstarch in any of the recipes in this book. If you prefer cornstarch to arrowroot, please feel free to experiment with substituting. When substituting cornstarch for arrowroot, you need to mix it with a small amount of liquid before adding it to whatever it is you are making, as it has a tendency to clump.

Other Dry Ingredients
Baking Powder

Not all baking powders are gluten-free. The following brands are, but if in doubt, make your own.

- Clabber Girl Baking Powder
- Davis Baking Powder
- Rumford Baking Powder, Aluminum-free
- Hain Pure Foods Featherweight Baking Powder
- Hearth Club Baking Powder
- Bob's Red Mill Baking Powder

To make your own baking powder, combine the following ingredients and store in an airtight container. To use in a recipe, replace 1½ teaspoons for every teaspoon of store-bought baking powder.

⅔ cup arrowroot

⅔ cup cream of tartar

⅓ cup baking soda

Flaxseeds

Flaxseeds are high in soluble fiber and an excellent source of omega-3 fatty acids. The seeds, like chia seeds, will add a spongy texture to baked goods and a nutty flavor.

Oats

Well, the debate over oats has finally come to an end. For many years, people with celiac disease and others who are gluten intolerant or sensitive struggled to know if the oats they purchased were contaminated with products containing gluten. Now the worry is over, as there are several companies providing dedicated facilities to bring us gluten-free oats! Yea! To date, I know of the following companies that sell gluten-free oats. There may be more available by the time you are reading this. The names of these companies are not ranked in any order of preference.

- Bob's Red Mill
- Cream Hill Estates
- FarmPure Foods
- Gluten Free Oats
- Gifts of Nature

Xanthan Gum and Guar Gum

Both xanthan gum and guar gum act as thickeners and binders of ingredients. Xanthan gum originates from a bacterium called *Xanthomonas campestris*. While I don't think consumption of small amounts of this product will hurt us, I have switched to guar gum in many of my recipes. Guar gum (powder or flakes) originates from the guar bean; it is cheaper to buy, and it achieves the same goal as xanthan gum.

I have made cookies both with and without guar gum or xanthan gum, but I have found that in muffins, breads, and scones, it behooves you to include a gum, as it really does help to keep the finished product from falling apart.

The general rule for either xanthan gum or guar gum is to use 1 teaspoon for each cup of flour for either yeasted breads or pizza dough. For quick breads or muffins, you should add in ½ teaspoon for each cup of flour.

Sweeteners

In the past, I have written sugar-free cookbooks (refined cane sugar). I sometimes used a fruit sweetener called Mixed Fruit Concentrate made by Mystic Lake Dairy, which is a combination of peach, pear, and pineapple purée (a fructose-based sweetener), or I used agave cactus nectar. Here are some other sweeteners you may wish to experiment with.

- Banana
- Applesauce
- Xylitol, a naturally occurring sugar alcohol found in some fruits, berries, and vegetables
- Dried fruit purée

Maple syrup: I have fallen in love with organic maple syrup, and you will notice that I use it quite often in my desserts! I decided to use maple syrup as the primary sweetener in this book. It is processed by boiling the sap from sugar maple trees to remove the water, and it is more natural than most sweeteners, as no chemicals are added. It is also low in saturated fat, cholesterol, and sodium and has small amounts of iron, calcium, niacin, biotin, folic acid, vitamin B, potassium, magnesium, phosphorus, and amino acids. That said, it too has its drawbacks. It is not a low-glycemic food, so it is not suitable for diabetics. I believe that maple syrup consumed in moderation is a great alternative to pure cane sugar. I also believe that maple syrup's vitamin and mineral content make it a viable alternative to agave cactus nectar.

Agave cactus nectar: Agave comes from several species of the agave plant, grown primarily in Mexico. Agave has a very mild taste, no aftertaste, and less is more, as it is very sweet. I would not recommend agave for diabetics, as emerging research has shown that while it is lower than other sweeteners on the glycemic index (a measure of how quickly it raises blood sugar levels), it is actually sweeter than table sugar. (Sweeter is not necessarily bad, as you can then use less in a recipe!)

In my cookbook *The Gluten-Free Vegan*, I used agave nectar as the primary sweetener in most of the dessert recipes. Over the past several months I have received e-mails from readers who were concerned about the information circulating on the Internet about the risks of agave. Having reviewed quite a bit of the literature, I have come to believe there is a difference between "commercialized agave nectar" and authentic organic agave nectar that is not processed with chemicals into a high-fructose product. If you are interested, I would recommend you read the following articles so you can decide for yourself.

"Agave Nectar Pros and Cons," by Cleo Libonati, RN, BSN, cofounder of Gluten Free Works, Inc. February, 11, 2011.
   http://glutenfreeworks.com/blog/2011/02/18/agave-nectar-pros-and-cons/

"Agave Syrup for Diabetics: Natural Sugar Substitute or Natural Fraud?"
   *http://www.naturaldiabetics.com/agave-syrup-diabetics-sugar
   -replacement-or-fraud/*

"Why Agave Nectar Is Not Worse Than High Fructose Corn Syrup," by Dr. Edward Group. April 5, 2010.
   http://www.globalhealingcenter.com/natural-health/agave-nectar/

I do continue to keep organic agave nectar in my pantry and use it in moderation. If you prefer agave and use a good, nonprocessed product, then feel free to use it in place of maple syrup when called for.

Stevia: I don't use this sweetener in this cookbook, despite the fact that it is considered by many to be the best healthy sugar alternative. Stevia is not a sugar. It is an herb that comes from the chrysanthemum family, and its leaves are used to make several types of sweeteners. Stevia is sold in both liquid and powdered form. I don't care much for the aftertaste or the texture of baked goods made with stevia. It has a glycemic index of less than 1, so I would encourage you to try working with it if you are diabetic or are looking for a truly low-GI alternative sweetener. There are several cookbooks on the market that use stevia exclusively, so if you are looking for a totally sugar-free option, this may be your best bet.

Brown rice syrup: Brown rice syrup is relatively low on the GI scale but it has some drawbacks, as it is dense and tends to make muffins and cakes too heavy. On the other hand, brown rice syrup works wonderfully in granola bars, or puffed rice cereal treats, as its stickiness helps to hold the ingredients together.

Blackstrap molasses: When white sugar is refined, it is stripped of all its nutrients. Blackstrap molasses is made up of all the nutrients that are removed from cane sugar. It is high in iron, calcium, magnesium, potassium, copper, and zinc. I love the flavor of molasses, and I like to use it in marinades. (Try the Portobello Mushroom Steak with Smothered Onions recipe found on page 140, or the Molasses Cookies found on page 182 that taste just like grandma used to make, but without the wheat flour and eggs!).

Raw sugar: This option is not much better than table sugar, as it is processed like white sugar (isn't that an interesting fact, when it is called "raw sugar,"), but it hasn't been as refined as white sugar. I do have to admit to using it on occasion, as I love the crunchy texture it provides, especially in a cookie recipe.

Organic sugar: This sugar is not assaulted with chemicals or pesticides, and it retains some of its darker color (molasses) because it is not processed to the same degree as cane sugar. I know I have said it before, but my mantra in this book, is MODERATION, MODERATION, MODERATION. If we all lived our lives doing everything in moderation, including eating, drinking, exercising, working, etc., we would be a healthier people. Let's remember that when using any sweetener in our cooking. I believe we can "cover up" the natural flavors and textures of a food by oversweetening it or by adding too much oil. Less is the ideal we are striving for.

Maple butter: I don't use this sweetener often—even though I love the flavor it provides—because it is quite expensive. If you haven't tried it and want to treat yourself, try Shady Maple Farms' certified organic maple butter. It is usually found in health food stores but you could also try buying it online. Besides being absolutely delicious, maple butter is a very condensed sweetener, so you don't need much. I truly love this sweetener, and when the holidays roll around, I splurge and buy it because it makes a wonderful gift.

Milks

Coconut, Hemp, Almond, Cashew, Brazil Nut, Macadamia, Hazelnut, Soy, Rice, and Seed Milks

I love homemade milk, but I don't always have the nuts on hand to make it, so I often use coconut milk in my recipes. If you wish to substitute a nut or seed milk for the coconut milk, I suggest going with a milk that will provide a thicker texture, such as cashew milk.

If you want to make your own nut or seed milks, you will need a good blender, a nut milk bag or cheesecloth, raw nuts or seeds, and purified water. Seed and nut milks are easy to make. The most important ingredient is time. You will want to set almonds aside in water overnight to get them soft enough to produce a delicious milk. Seeds like sesame or sunflower take less time to soak, only four hours or so. You don't need to soak macadamia nuts at all, but I recommend soaking cashews for at least four to six hours at the minimum. I usually just soak them overnight and then make the milk first thing when I get up. You can also experiment with combining the nuts with seeds, such as a cashew and sesame seed milk.

If you don't have a nut milk bag or sprout bag, use cheesecloth. I find I can stretch a package of recycled cheesecloth a long way by unfolding it fully and then cutting a small piece of cloth that will adequately cover the bowl I am pouring the milk into. To make your own nut milk, do the following:

1. Place 1 cup raw nuts in a large bowl and cover with 4 cups of purified water.

2. Soak the nuts overnight (almonds, cashews, Brazil nuts, etc.) (4 hours or more).

3. In the morning, pour the water and nuts into a blender. Purée on high until the mixture is completely blended, and you can see the water has turned white.

4. Place a piece of cheesecloth over a sieve placed over the top of the bowl you soaked the nuts in, and pour the blended mixture through the cheesecloth. You don't pour it all at once, as it must drain through the cheesecloth, so go slowly. After the milk drains through, add some more of the blended mixture, until all of it has passed through the cheesecloth. I squeeze out the cheesecloth, so I get every bit of the milk.

5. Next, put the milk mixture back into the blender and place 1 or 2 drops of vanilla, if desired, into the blender, or add a pinch of agave or maple syrup, and blend together. This is heavenly! Place the milk into a quart jar and keep in the refrigerator until needed. It will last up to a week if kept in the fridge. Experiment with this, and you may never want to drink store-bought "milks" again!

Vegan Cheeses

I must admit that cheese is a challenge to replace in recipes, as I want the alternatives to produce the same results as cow cheese and that's really not realistic. I have searched and searched for good cheese alternatives and here are my favorites.

Galaxy Foods, rice cheese, mozzarella flavor. This cheese is gluten-free, nut-free, and soy-free. It also comes in other flavors, but I use this one in my favorite lasagna recipe, and it works very well.

WayFare Foods has come out with a line of dairy-free, soy-free cheese alternatives that are made from whole grain, certified gluten–free oatmeal. The flavors include Cheddar-Style Spread, Hickory-Smoked Cheddar-Style Spread, Mexi Cheddar-Style Dip, and Cheddar-Style Dip. The hickory cheddar is my favorite, and it's great for grilled cheese sandwiches or in countless other recipes.

Follow Your Heart has a full line of gluten-free, dairy-free cheeses. Their cheeses melt well but do not have an overpowering flavor. I have used this company's nacho cheese, mozzarella, and jack cheese alternatives. They also produce nice cream cheese and sour cream alternatives.

Egg Replacers

My newest favorite egg replacer is chia seeds. I just love the way these seeds turn into the same texture as an egg when mixed with water. Chia seeds are, as I mentioned previously, one of the richest plant sources of omega-3 fatty acids, and they are chock full of fiber too. They don't have an overpowering flavor, so you don't have to worry about that in your recipes, but they do add just a wee bit of crunch, which I love. I hope you enjoy the French Toast recipe in this cookbook as much as I do; it is made with chia seeds in place of eggs. See the recipe on page 38.

Sometimes I use ¼ cup mashed banana in place of 1 egg in recipes, and I also use the same amount of applesauce to replace 1 egg.

Of course, flaxseeds mixed with water is another great standby, as are powdered egg replacers, such as Ener-G Foods or Bob's Red Mill.

When using Energ-G Foods egg replacer, follow the directions on the box: to replace 1 egg, whisk 2 tablespoons warm water with 1½ teaspoons of the powder; whisk together until light and bubbly. Of course you would double that if you wanted to replace 2 eggs. I sometimes use a combination of Ener-G for 1 egg and chia seeds mixed with water, or ¼ cup of banana for the second egg. Play around with this—there are, I am sure, other possibilities!

Margarine, Palm Shortening, and Oils

Earth Balance is a brand of margarine that I frequently use because it is GMO-free, trans fat–free, and contains no hydrogenated oils or cholesterol. The Buttery Spread margarine also comes in a soy-free version made with palm fruit, canola, safflower, olive oil, and pea protein. However, if you have an allergy to corn, or wish to avoid corn, this is not a viable option for you. If that is the case, I highly recommend organic, virgin coconut oil.

Virgin coconut oil remains a good substitution for soy-based margarines, and in some cases, so does palm shortening. There are a few manufacturers of palm shortening, but my favorite is Spectrum. It is made from 100 percent organic, expeller-pressed palm oil. It comes in an economical twenty-four-ounce tub that seems to last forever! It is great for piecrusts and cookies. It can be stored in your cupboard as it does not require refrigeration.

I use olive oil, grapeseed oil, canola oil, and coconut oil in this cookbook. I like olive oil, as it is high in monounsaturated fats, unlike many oils that are high in trans fats or saturated fats. Monounsaturated fats reduce the risk for heart disease by lowering LDL, which is the "bad" cholesterol level in the blood. I use only extra virgin or organic cold–pressed virgin olive oils as they are the least processed and better for you. Whatever your choice for butter substitutes, be sure to stay away from partially hydro-genated oils!

You can often use less oil to produce the same effect when sautéing foods or sauté a veggie broth. If you would like to research the health benefits of omitting oils from your diet, I would recommend reading *Prevent and Reverse Heart Disease: The Revolutionary, Scientifically Proven, Nutrition-Based Cure*, by Caldwell B. Esselstyn Jr., MD.

Cooking with Wine

I often use wine when cooking. Sometimes I will sauté vegetables in wine, other times I will use wine as a flavor enhancer in sauces. In this cookbook, I recommend wines based on their characteristics, giving you an example of a wine that will work in the recipe, but also allowing you to select according to your own tastes and preferences. For example, in the Eggplant Parmesan recipe (page 130), I suggest a full-bodied red wine, with hints of blackberry and blueberry, such as a Cabernet. You could also use a Syrah or a Pinot Noir, and the recipe would work just as well. Remember, the wine you don't use in the recipe is fair game for the cook to drink!

I used my favorite Pacific Northwest wines in many of these recipes. They come from Chatter Creek Winery, in Woodinville, Washington. I don't recommend cooking with cheap "cooking wines" you find in the supermarket in the condiment aisle as these are often flavorless, and they do not add the richness that one is looking for.

Organic Wines

There are several organic wines available in the United States. These wines are made using organic, biodynamic practices. If you prefer to cook and drink only organic wines, here is a list of some that recently were rated by *Wine Spectator* on a 100-point scale to be quite good.

WHITES

Bonterra Chardonnay received a rating of 87 points.
WillaKenzie Pinot Blanc received a rating of 90 points.
Pacific Rim Riesling received a rating of 87 points.

REDS

Tablas Creek Cotes received a rating of 88 points.
Maysara Pinot Noir received 91 points.
Snoqualmie Syrah received 87 points.

I hope you will experiment with wines in your recipes. The cooking process always removes the alcohol from the dish, and what is left after the alcohol burns off is the delicious flavor that enlivens the flavors of your creations.

If you do not want to use wines in the recipes, please feel free to either omit it entirely or substitute white grape juice, vegetable broth, or water.

The Importance of Organic Fruits and Vegetables

Over the past several decades our foods have been bombarded with chemicals, pesticides, hormones, and antibiotics. If you have read the book *Food, Inc.* or have seen the documentary film, you know that there are reasons to worry about the foods we eat. Europe and many other countries do not allow genetically modified foods or certain pesticides on fruits and veggies, but here in the United States, it's all about growing more food, making it last longer on the shelves, and finding ways to develop pest-resistant seeds. But at what cost?

Pesticides especially may pose dangers for children between the ages of one and eleven. According to a 2006 study (U.S. EPA: "A Framework for Assessing Health Risk of Environmental Exposures to Children") conducted by the National Academy of Sciences and the Environmental Working Group, infants and children were at high risk for cancer due to exposure to carcinogenic pesticides. The overly early development of prepubescent girls and boys and the increase in asthma and other respiratory diseases may be related to the pesticides, hormones, and other chemicals that are added to our foods. I hope you will consider reading the articles and checking out the resources I list below or others on the subject.

"Pesticides and Food: Why Children May Be Especially Sensitive to Pesticides." *www.epa.gov/pesticides/food/pest.htm.*

"Pesticides and Food: Health Problems Pesticides May Pose." *http://www.epa.gov/opp00001/food/risks.htm.* This site also provides links to other resources, such as the "Human Health Risk Assessment,"

"Registration and Chemical-Specific Information," and "Citizen's Guide to Pest Control and Pesticide Safety."

"Chemicals in Food Raise Children's Cancer Toll," Samuel S. Epstein, MD, and Ralph W. Moss, *New York Times* letter, July 16, 1991.

Cancer Prevention Coalition. *http://www.preventcancer.com*

"10 Reasons to Eat Organic," by Andrew Weil, MD. *www.drweil.com*

"Pesticides in the Air, Kids at Risk." *http://earthjustice.org*

Soil Association: *http://www.soilassociation.org*

Genetically Modified (GMO) Foods

Genetically modified foods (commonly referred to as "GMO foods") are derived from genetically modified organisms. Specific changes are introduced into their DNA by genetic engineering techniques, including selective breeding, plant breeding, and mutation breeding. The most common GM foods are soybeans, corn, cottonseed oil, rice, papayas, and canola.

I highly encourage you to avoid GM foods and to look for the words "GMO free" when purchasing ingredients from the market. The main concerns include safety issues, ecological impact on our planet, and the loss of "real" foods from our farms and communities. One of the worst things is the loss of heirloom seeds. ALL of our seeds will soon be contaminated whether we like it or not! We will soon have no non-GMO seeds available. Research in Europe has reported some DNA damage to protein levels in genes with GM foods. (See "Monsanto Whistleblower Says Genetically Engineered Crops May Cause Disease," by Jeffrey M. Smith. www.globalresearch.ca/index.php. November 19, 2006,)

You can avoid GM foods by shopping your farmers' markets and local food co-ops, buying organic foods (if a food is certified organic, it is not genetically modified) and whole foods, preparing your meals from scratch, and educating yourself about GM foods. Be sure to educate yourself on the risks or benefits by reading all that you can. I also recommend the films *The Future of Food* and *Food, Inc.* Our children are our future—let's feed them wholesome foods, not genetically modified foods.

Farmers' Markets and Food Co-ops

A gluten-free vegan kitchen should begin with fresh fruits and vegetables purchased at your local farmers' market or through other means of gathering the freshest produce available.

I believe in buying food as close to home as possible and supporting local farmers' markets, food co-ops, and grocers. Why do we need to eat apples grown in New Zealand? If they are out of season here, let's wait until they are in season. Think how much more we will appreciate fruit, if we wait and bite into a truly fresh piece of fruit grown locally.

Where I live, we are fortunate to have local farmers who provide their produce either at a local neighborhood market or through an open farm where we can buy directly from the farmer. You can also join food co-ops and have wonderful weekly, biweekly, or monthly baskets of fresh produce delivered to your front door. There are so many options available to ensure that the foods you eat come directly from the source from which they were grown, as quickly as possible. I hope you will search out and check out, if you haven't already, your local fresh markets. Depending on where you live, you may have farmers' markets available to you all year long. When I visit Kauai, there is a farmers' market in a different town every day. I love going from one small town to another to see what each area has to offer. Many growers offer produce not commonly found at your neighborhood grocery. There are resources available online to find farmers' markets in your area. You might check out one of these, or check with your local chamber of commerce.

USDA Agricultural Marketing Service website. This site maintains a listing of farmers' markets across the United States.

You submit your zip code, and it will list all of the markets within a specific mile radius. Their website is: *http://search.ams.usda.gov/farmersmarkets.*

http://www.localharvest.org/. This site provides you with information on where to find organic farmers' markets in your area, local family farm information, sustainably grown foods, and so much more. I love this website. They also provide a newsletter, blog information, and a listing of events taking place around the country.

So, what foods are the "absolute" musts to buy organic? This list of foods frequently contaminated with pesticides was derived from the Environmental Working Group:

- Apples
- Bell peppers
- Blueberries
- Carrots
- Celery
- Cherries
- Imported grapes

- Kale /collard greens
- Lettuce
- Peaches
- Pears
- Potatoes
- Nectarines
- Strawberries

All other fruits and veggies are considered "clean," and you don't need to purchase organic unless you wish to. I myself prefer to eat as much organic as I can.

During the winter months when fresh vegetables are not available, such as tomatoes, I sometimes reach for the organic canned versions in the market. I want to know that the canned items I am resorting to are also organic and have not been treated with pesticides or other chemicals. Note also that many canned tomato sauces actually list "wheat" on the label. It is used as a thickener, so be sure you read the labels and stick to organic as much as you can.

I hope you have found the information provided in this book to be of help to you. I couldn't simply write a comfort food cookbook without taking into consideration our collective well-being. May we pass on to our friends and family the intention to eat foods that taste good and nourish our spirits, and may we also be mindful of how these foods support our bodies and our planet.

Get Your Morning Going!
Ideas for Breakfast

Amaranth, Get Set, and GO!

THIS IS BY FAR my favorite breakfast cereal. It is super easy to make, fills you up, gives you incredible energy to take on the world (OK, maybe just the day), and it is good for you! Why not give it a try? I make this at least four times per week, and I love it with a dash of cinnamon, a chopped apple, a handful of fresh berries, and a couple of chopped dates or dried figs. You can experiment with the recipe—there's a ton you can do with it—and see what works for you. Get creative!

Ok, you get the picture . . . there is a lot you can add to this breakfast grain to give it more UMPH and dress it up!

1. Place a saucepan on the stove and add the water and amaranth seed. Heat to boiling and then reduce the heat to medium-low, just so the water simmers, cooking the amaranth seed about 20 minutes, or until thick.

2. Remove from the heat and add cardamom, cinnamon, dates, nuts, or whatever you wish before serving. You can also add a nondairy milk and organic maple syrup if desired. Serve hot.

SERVES 4

2 ½ cups water
1 cup amaranth seed

Optional Add-ins
Chopped apple
Banana
Berries
Cardamom
Cinnamon
Chia seeds
Dried fruits
Nondairy milk
Maple syrup
Nuts
Strawberry Applesauce
   (page 47)

Banana-Buckwheat Pancakes

3 teaspoons Ener-G egg
  replacer

4 tablespoons warm water

2 to 3 tablespoons
  grapeseed or canola oil
  (or vegetable spray) plus
  more for cooking

1 ½ cups So Delicious
  coconut milk or other milk

2 tablespoons agave cactus
  nectar

¼ cup applesauce,
  unsweetened

¾ cup buckwheat flour

½ cup brown rice flour

2 teaspoons baking powder

1 teaspoon cinnamon

¼ cup mashed banana

¼ cup chopped pecans

WHAT A GREAT WAY to start your day! These pancakes will fill you up and power your morning. I like to add blueberries to the mixture, and if I do that, I usually don't add the nuts. You can serve these with a nut butter, organic maple syrup, jam, coconut yogurt, applesauce, or whatever you prefer.

1. In a medium-size bowl, whisk together the egg replacer and the warm water. Beat with a whisk until the mixture is light and bubbly. Add the oil, milk, agave, and applesauce and stir together really well. (If you prefer less fat, use only 2 tablespoons of the oil. If the batter seems too dry, you can add in 1 to 2 additional tablespoons of applesauce.)

2. In a separate bowl, combine the flours, baking powder, and cinnamon to blend well. Add the dry ingredients to the wet ingredients and then carefully fold in the banana and pecans, being careful not to overbeat the mixture.

3. Heat a skillet to medium-high heat and add a small amount of the canola oil or vegetable spray. When it is hot, add a ladle full of batter (about ¼ cup) to the skillet and cook until bubbles appear on the pancake. Flip the pancake over and cook a few minutes on the other side. Continue this process until you have cooked all of the pancakes and everyone has been served.

4. If there is any batter left over, you can store it in an airtight container in the refrigerator for 2 to 3 days.

Banana-Nut Bread

A GREAT WAY TO USE up any ripe bananas and a GREAT snack for the kids to take to school, have with breakfast, or eat as an after-school snack. This is also a terrific bread to serve to guests or just enjoy with a hot cup of tea.

1. Preheat the oven to 350°F. Grease and flour a standard bread pan.

2. In a large mixing bowl, beat together the canola oil, maple syrup, sugar, vanilla, and applesauce. Mash bananas with a fork, and then add to the mixture, stirring well to combine.

3. In a small bowl, combine the dry ingredients and stir well.

4. Incorporate the dry ingredients with the wet ingredients and beat 30 seconds, or until the batter is well blended. Fold in walnuts.

5. Pour the batter into the prepared pan and bake for 40 to 45 minutes. Check the center of the bread for doneness by inserting a toothpick, which when removed, should be completely clean. Let stand on a wire rack for 10 minutes before removing the bread from the pan.

MAKES 1 LOAF

¼ cup canola oil

½ cup maple syrup

¼ cup sugar

1 teaspoon vanilla

¼ cup organic chunky applesauce

2 ripe bananas, mashed

¼ cup coconut or sorghum flour

1¼ cups all-purpose gluten-free flour

½ teaspoon salt

2 teaspoons baking powder

1 teaspoon baking soda

1 teaspoon xanthan gum

1 teaspoon cinnamon

Pinch of cardamom, optional

½ cup chopped walnuts

Cinnamon-Oat Scones

MAKES 8 SCONES

½ cup oats

¾ cup tapioca flour

1 cup sorghum flour

½ cup brown rice flour

½ cup potato starch

¼ teaspoon sea salt

1 ½ teaspoons cinnamon

1 teaspoon baking soda

4 teaspoons baking powder

½ teaspoon guar gum

⅓ cup plus 1 tablespoon
   organic coconut oil

1 cup So Delicious coconut
   milk (soy or hemp milk will
   also work)

¼ cup maple syrup

THESE SCONES do not rise very high because they are made with heavier grains, but my taste testers all liked them just the same. Someone said they would be great with coffee or tea, and another said they would also be good with a dollop of jam. And some liked them just the way they were!

1. Preheat the oven to 400°F. Line a cookie sheet with parchment paper.

2. Place the dry ingredients in a large bowl and stir together until mixed. Cut in the coconut oil (expeller-pressed coconut oil is a solid, not a liquid) with a pastry cutter or fork until it is incorporated and you do not see little balls of coconut oil. Add in the milk and maple syrup and stir until you can gather all of the ingredients together.

3. Place a large piece of waxed paper on a work surface and turn the oat mixture out on the surface and press it out into a large circle about ½ inch thick. Cut into 8 scones (I think of it as a pie, and cut the mixture in half, then in half again, and once again until I have 8 equal scones).

4. Lay the scones out like cookies on the prepared sheet. Bake at 400°F for 12 to 14 minutes. Cool on a wire rack. Store in an airtight container.

Dried Cherry Granola

I HAVE MADE this granola for several people, and they all wanted the recipe. I even have a friend on the East Coast I ship this granola to. Her name is Susan, and she loves it so much she trades me her precious New England maple syrup for my granola. Need I say more?

1. Preheat the oven to 325°F. Lightly spray a large baking sheet with canola oil.

2. Place all of the ingredients into a large bowl and stir together really well with either a wooden spoon or clean hands, and then pour the mixture onto the prepared pan and spread it out evenly.

3. Bake for 25 to 30 minutes, stirring the mixture every 10 minutes to ensure it does not burn. The granola will be browned when it is done; it will be soft when it first comes out of the oven but it will become crunchy as it cools.

4. Cool on a wire rack. Store the granola in an airtight container.

2 cups puffed rice
¼ cup coconut flour, or finely ground, shredded unsweetened coconut flakes
½ cup pumpkin seeds
½ cup chopped dried cherries
1 tablespoon almond meal
1 tablespoon chia seeds
1 cup chopped walnuts
1 cup chopped cashews
¼ cup organic peanut butter (or cashew butter or almond butter)
¼ cup canola oil
½ cup organic maple syrup
¼ teaspoon vanilla
1 teaspoon cinnamon
Pinch of salt
Pinch of cardamom

French Toast

4 teaspoons chia seeds

8 tablespoons water

4 tablespoons well-mashed banana (optional)

4 tablespoons So Delicious coconut milk

Dash of vanilla

¼ teaspoon cinnamon (more if you prefer)

4 slices of vegan, gluten-free bread

3 to 4 teaspoons vegan margarine or canola oil

THIS IS OBVIOUSLY not your traditional French toast, but I love it. I actually had it this morning, while I was typing up recipes. While the optional mashed banana makes the bread a bit mushy, the taste is divine! This recipe serves only two, so if you have a crowd, you will need to increase all of the ingredients to accommodate. It takes very little time to make this dish, and it can easily be adapted to serve more.

1. In a small casserole dish, whisk the chia seeds together really well with the water and let the mixture sit for about 5 to 10 minutes. This allows the mixture to thicken. If you are using banana in this recipe, mash it really well with a fork on a plate and add to the chia mixture. Then add the milk, vanilla, and cinnamon to the chia mixture and place your bread in the mixture to soak, turning over once so that both sides of the bread are covered with the mixture.

2. Heat a large skillet to medium-high and add the margarine. When it is hot, transfer the bread to the pan and cook for about 3 to 4 minutes on each side. The French toast will not brown like traditional French toast, but if you omit the banana, it will be crunchy like nonvegan French toast. The addition of banana is delicious, but it definitely keeps the bread softer. I don't mind that, as the flavors are what I enjoy most.

3. If you do want a crunchier French toast, let it cook longer on each side. Serve hot with your choice of organic maple syrup, fresh Strawberry Applesauce (see recipe on page 47), jam, nut butters, or your own favorite toppings.

Good Morning Sunshine Grains

SERVES 4

2 cups water

⅓ cup quinoa, rinsed well
and drained

⅓ cup gluten-free oats

⅓ cup millet, rinsed and
drained

Optional Toppings

½ teaspoon cinnamon

Chopped dates or raisins

Chopped cashews, walnuts,
pecans

Chia seeds, flaxseed meal, or
flaxseeds

Organic maple syrup (1 to
2 tablespoons), brown rice
syrup, or agave nectar

Milk (coconut, almond, rice,
hemp, or soy)

Berries (blueberries,
raspberries, strawberries,
marionberries,
huckleberries)

Fresh fruit, such as banana,
chopped apple, peaches,
pineapple, nectarines,
mango

Cranberry-Apple Chutney
(found on page 54)

I LOVE THE combination of multiple grains in this recipe. Breakfast, while comforting, should also be invigorating, to get the brain fueled up for the day. Adding one or more toppings to this hot cereal will fill up your gas tank for the day and sustain you for several hours.

1. Place the water and grains in a stockpot and bring to a boil. Reduce the heat to medium-low and cover. Simmer grains until cooked, about 15 minutes.

2. Serve with your choice of toppings.

Oat and Ginger Granola

NOW THAT GLUTEN-FREE oats are available, I thought I would make a granola using them. This one has candied ginger in it, which gives it a nice flavor. Feel free to add more ginger if you would like it to have a more prominent presence. Also, to go along with the ginger theme, a hint of cardamom is really nice in this recipe.

1. Preheat the oven to 325°F.

2. In a large bowl, combine the ingredients, mixing thoroughly. Evenly spread the granola onto a baking sheet and bake, stirring often, for about 30 minutes or until golden brown.

3. This granola stores really nicely in an airtight container for at least 1 week.

3 cups gluten-free oats

1 tablespoon chia seeds or almond meal

2 tablespoons sorghum flour (rice flour may substitute)

1 teaspoon cinnamon

¼ teaspoon cardamom

1 tablespoon shredded coconut

¼ cup chopped pecans

1 cup chopped cashews

½ cup chopped walnuts

¾ to 1 cup raisins (optional)

¼ cup chopped candied ginger

¼ cup pumpkin seeds

½ teaspoon sea salt

¼ cup canola oil

½ cup brown rice syrup

Peach and Blueberry
Protein Smoothie

SERVES 4

1 scoop protein powder

2 cups milk substitute

1 tablespoon chia seeds

1 tablespoon flaxseeds

4 cups organic blueberries

½ cup organic peaches

1 tablespoon maple syrup

Ice (optional)

Mint leaves for garnish

PROTEIN = ENERGY. Smoothie = Delicious. This recipe is chock full of both! The fruit you use can be fresh or frozen, and ice can be added as desired. For a protein powder I use Life's Basics Plant Protein by Lifetime, and for a milk substitute I use So Delicious coconut milk.

1. Using a blender, combine the ingredients, mix, and serve. Top with a sprig of fresh mint to jazz it up.

Poppy Seed Muffins

IMAGINE INSTEAD of that beautiful sea of red poppies in *The Wizard of Oz*, a big plate of warm muffins! The Wicked Witch of the West wishes she had this recipe. I might be stretching it a little, but these muffins will definitely leave you tapping your ruby slippers.

1. Preheat the oven to 350°F. Grease and flour a muffin tin.

2. Grind the poppy seeds in a blender or coffee grinder.

3. In a saucepan, combine the poppy seeds and coconut milk and bring to a boil. Remove from heat, whisk in the egg replacer until fully incorporated, then set aside.

4. In a large mixing bowl, using an electric mixer, beat the palm shortening, coconut oil, sugar, and maple syrup on high until fluffy. Then, one at a time, add the vanilla, the poppy seed–coconut milk mixture, yogurt, applesauce, and lemon juice, stirring to fully incorporate each ingredient before adding the next.

5. In another large bowl, sift together the dry ingredients, then slowly add these to the wet ingredients. Do not overbeat.

6. Spoon the batter into the prepared muffin tin. Bake 20 to 30 minutes and cool on a wire rack.

MAKES 12 MUFFINS

½ cup plus 1 tablespoon poppy seeds

1 cup coconut milk

1 tablespoon egg replacer

½ cup organic palm shortening (Spectrum)

½ cup organic coconut oil

¼ cup organic sugar

½ cup organic maple syrup

2 teaspoons vanilla

½ cup So Delicious vanilla yogurt

¼ cup chunky applesauce

2 tablespoons lemon juice (optional)

¼ cup coconut flour

1¾ cups Bob's Red Mill All Purpose Gluten-Free Flour

1 teaspoon xanthan gum

2 teaspoons baking powder

½ teaspoon salt

Pumpkin Waffles

1½ teaspoons egg replacer
(such as Ener-G Foods or
Bob's Red Mill)

2 tablespoons warm water

¾ cup milk, So Delicious
(hemp, soy, nut, or rice)

¼ cup organic canned
pumpkin

2 tablespoons canola oil

¾ cup sorghum flour

¼ cup potato starch

¼ cup tapioca flour

2 teaspoons baking powder

2 teaspoons cinnamon

¼ teaspoon ginger

Pinch of nutmeg

Pinch of salt

2 tablespoons chopped
pecans (optional)

Vegetable oil or nonstick
cooking spray

WAFFLES FROM SCRATCH are always a crowd pleaser, morning, noon, and night! Add pumpkin and a little spice, and you've got an instant classic. To really take them over the top, try a dollop of Maple-Pumpkin Butter from page 204.

This recipe can be doubled and the batter stored in the freezer for later use.

1. Preheat the waffle iron.

2. In a large mixing bowl, whisk the egg replacer with warm water. Add nondairy milk, pumpkin, and canola oil.

3. In a small bowl, combine the dry ingredients. Using a sieve to sift in the flours and the starch will lead to fewer clumps and a fluffier batter.

4. Add the dry ingredients to the wet ingredients; incorporate the dry ingredients until thoroughly combined, but do not overmix. Stir in optional pecans.

5. When the waffle iron is hot, spray with vegetable oil and add 1 ladle full of batter to each griddle. Cook until golden brown, according to waffle iron manufacturer instructions.

6. Serve with your choice of toppings.

Raw Cinnamon Rolls

THESE TAKE A BIT OF WORK and an open mind, as they are not your traditional cinnamon rolls. While the dough was chilling, I found myself coming back for small bites, over and over again. Might as well have just sliced off a bit of the roll and called it a day! These can be jazzed up with Peanut Butter Frosting (found on page 202) or cashew cream. This recipe takes about one and a half hours to make.

1. Place the walnuts and cashews in a food processor and pulse until finely ground. Transfer them to a large bowl.

2. Wash the food processor bowl and then add in the dates, chia seeds, flaxseeds, water, and vanilla. Pulse until the mixture makes a paste.

3. Remove this mixture from the food processor and separate it in half, placing half of the mixture into the large bowl with the nuts. Add the maple syrup, oil, cardamom, 1 tablespoon of the cinnamon, and a dash of sea salt to the mixture in the large bowl. Stir to mix together really well. This nut mixture will become the "dough" for your cinnamon rolls.

4. Add the rest of the cinnamon to the other half of the mixture, return it to the food processor, and pulse until smooth. This paste will become your "filling" for the cinnamon rolls.

(continues)

MAKES 6 TO 8 ROLLS

1½ cups raw walnuts
¼ cup cashews
1 cup pitted and chopped Medjool dates
½ cup chia seeds
1 cup flaxseeds
¼ cup water
1 teaspoon vanilla
2 tablespoons organic maple syrup
2 tablespoons coconut oil or canola oil
¼ teaspoon cardamom
1½ tablespoons cinnamon, divided
Dash of sea salt

Raw Cinnamon Rolls *(continued)*

5. Lay a piece of waxed or parchment paper out on a work surface and then form the nut mixture into a square on the paper, about ¼ inch thick. Carefully spread the paste over the top of the nut mixture and spread it out evenly over the entire surface. Using the paper as a mechanism to roll up the mixture, carefully roll it up, forming a tight roll.

6. Place it in the refrigerator for about an hour to chill and then slice it into 6 to 8 even pieces for serving. You can, as I mentioned, top with frosting, orange icing, or cashew frosting, but I personally think these are sweet enough as they are.

Strawberry Applesauce

BERRIES ARE one of my favorite foods—I prefer them to chocolate any day. I also love fresh applesauce, so this was a natural combination for me. If you want to use other berries in this recipe, feel free. Marionberries would be delicious, as would raspberries, or if you want to divert even further, consider rhubarb. If you decide to use fresh rhubarb, you may wish to adjust the sweetness, as rhubarb is a tart fruit.

1. In a large stockpot, bring apples, berries, and water to a boil. Stir in maple syrup, reduce heat, and cook over very low heat until fruit is soft and thick, about 1 hour.

2. Add spices, vanilla, and lemon juice. The sauce can be left chunky and served as a compote or puréed in a food processor until smooth.

3. Store in a jar in the fridge for up to one week.

MAKES 3½ CUPS

5 cups cored and chopped Granny Smith or other organic apple
2 cups fresh or frozen strawberries
½ cup water
½ cup maple syrup
½ teaspoon cinnamon
¼ teaspoon cardamom
½ teaspoon vanilla extract
1 tablespoon lemon juice

Pumpkin Bread

MAKES 1 LOAF

½ cup canola oil

¼ cup organic sugar

¼ cup maple syrup

¼ cup applesauce

1 teaspoon vanilla

3 teaspoons Ener-G egg replacer, mixed with 4 tablespoons warm water until frothy

¾ cup pumpkin, canned or fresh

1 ½ cups sorghum flour (or brown rice flour)

½ cup coconut flour

2 teaspoons baking powder

1 teaspoon baking soda

½ teaspoon salt

½ teaspoon grated nutmeg

1 teaspoon cinnamon

½ cup chopped pecans

½ cup pitted and chopped dates

THIS BREAD won't last long around your house. The recipe makes one large loaf, but you will wish you had two! I never frost this bread; it does not need it. Your kids will love it, you will love it, and if you are not careful, your neighbors will love it. If you are worried about the fat in this recipe, cut the oil in half and double the applesauce. My goal in developing these recipes was to create delicious, comforting foods, but I also want you to take care of your health! This simple switch will not negatively affect the bread.

1. Preheat the oven to 350°F. Grease and flour a bread pan.

2. In a large mixer or mixing bowl, beat the oil, sugar, and maple syrup on high until well mixed. Reduce the mixer speed to medium and add applesauce, vanilla, and egg replacer, and beat for 1 minute. Incorporate a heaping ¾ cup pumpkin into the wet ingredients until blended.

3. In a smaller bowl, combine dry ingredients and slowly add to the batter. Stir in the dates and nuts, before pouring batter into the prepared bread pan.

4. Bake for 45 to 50 minutes, or until a toothpick inserted into the center of the loaf can be cleanly removed. Cool on a wire rack for 10 minutes in the pan, then remove bread from the pan and continue to cool on wire rack.

Scrambled Tofu and Vegetables

THIS RECIPE is super simple but takes about one and a half hours, including marinating time. I make up a batch of the marinade and keep it in the fridge. I soak the tofu in the marinade for about one hour, but you don't have to wait that long. You could also marinate it overnight if that works better for you. Be sure to drain the tofu on paper towels before adding it to the vegetables.

1. Mix together the ¼ cup olive oil, wine, garlic, tamarind sauce, molasses, sea salt, and balsamic vinegar in an 8 x 8-inch casserole dish. Whisk this mixture together well, then crumble the drained tofu into the mixture and set aside to marinate.

2. Heat a large skillet to medium-high heat and add the tablespoon of olive oil. Sauté the onion until soft, about 4 minutes. Add the broccolini and continue to cook, stirring frequently, for 5 to 7 minutes. Add in the mushrooms and peppers and cook until the mushrooms begin to release their juices, about 3 to 4 minutes.

3. Drain the marinated tofu and add it to the skillet. Add in the basil and stir to mix. Season with salt and pepper to taste. Heat through and serve immediately.

Note: You can also use the veggie broth in place of some oil.

SERVES 4

¼ cup plus 1 tablespoon olive oil, divided

2 tablespoons red wine (optional)

1 to 2 cloves garlic, minced

1 teaspoon tamarind sauce

½ teaspoon molasses

¼ teaspoon sea salt

1 teaspoon balsamic vinegar

1 (12.3-ounce) package Nori firm tofu, drained

1 cup chopped onion

2 cups chopped broccolini or broccoli

2 cups cleaned, sliced mushrooms, stems removed

¼ cup chopped piquanté peppers or red bell peppers

2 to 4 tablespoons torn fresh basil

½ teaspoon fresh cracked pepper

¼ teaspoon sea salt (optional)

Snacks and Party Favorites

Bruschetta

NOTHING BEATS A SLICE of homemade bruschetta on the deck with a cool beverage! I love this recipe. If you don't have any fresh salsa in the house, use sliced tomatoes; they will work just fine too. I like salsa because it adds some spice, but you can add a pinch of cayenne pepper to the tomatoes or some chipotle pepper and achieve the same result.

1. Turn your broiler on high. Place the slices of bread directly on the rack in the oven and toast the bread on both sides until browned. Remove from the oven and place the bread on a cookie sheet.

2. Add 1 tablespoon of salsa to each slice of bread, followed by 4 to 5 fresh basil leaves and then lay a thin layer of the mozzarella cheese over the top of each slice of bread. Sprinkle the tops of each with fresh cracked pepper and broil in the oven until the cheese melts. Cut each slice of bread in half or into triangles.

SERVES 4 OR MORE

4 slices vegan, gluten-free bread (see Millet Bread on page 101)
4 tablespoons fresh salsa
12 to 15 fresh basil leaves, or more, if desired
4 slices or more (up to 4 ounces) vegan mozzarella cheese, cut into thin strips (I like Follow Your Heart brand, but rice cheese is also good in this recipe)
Fresh cracked pepper

Cranberry-Apple Chutney

MAKES 4 TO 5 CUPS

2 crisp organic apples, cut
   into cubes (about 4 cups)
¼ cup raisins
¼ cup pitted and chopped
   Medjool dates
½ cup raw chopped pecans
3 tablespoons vegan
   margarine, melted
1 cup peeled and chopped
   fresh orange
⅛ cup lemon juice
⅓ to ½ cup apple cider
½ cup organic maple syrup
1 teaspoon ground ginger
½ teaspoon cinnamon
2 cups whole cranberries,
   fresh or frozen

EXCELLENT AS an accompaniment to veggies, delicious in oatmeal, over coconut ice cream, or stuffed into baked apples, this is a sweet and tangy topper! You can make this chutney way ahead of time, store it in the fridge, and serve it hot or cold.

1. Preheat the oven to 400°F. In a large mixing bowl, combine all of the ingredients except the cranberries and stir well. Pour the mixture into a 9 x 9-inch baking dish and bake for 1 hour. Be sure to stir the chutney every 20 minutes or so to ensure even cooking.

2. Remove the chutney from the oven and add the cranberries. Return it to the oven and bake an additional 20 to 25 minutes. Let cool.

Guacamole

THIS IS ONE of my favorite snacks. You can put guacamole on a number of things, including roasted acorn squash, baked yams, bean dishes, and enchiladas, and it's great stuffed in tomatoes or piquant peppers too!

1. Chop the onion, garlic, red bell pepper, and tomato and place in a large bowl. Mash the avocados with a fork and then squeeze the lime over the top and add the chopped cilantro and cumin. Add salt and pepper to taste and mix together well.

2. Place one of the avocado pits in the bowl to avoid browning. Cover the guacamole and refrigerate until ready to serve.

MAKES 1½ CUPS

¼ cup finely chopped red onion

1 teaspoon finely chopped garlic

¼ cup finely chopped red bell pepper

¾ cup fresh coarsely chopped tomato

2 large avocados, peeled, pitted, and cut into chunks

1 tablespoon plus 1 teaspoon fresh lime juice

¼ cup chopped cilantro, stems removed

1 teaspoon cumin

Salt and pepper to taste

Pico de Gallo Salsa

MAKES A LOT!

4 cups de-seeded tomatoes

1 cup red finely diced onion

¼ cup finely diced jalapeño pepper

1 tablespoon finely diced garlic

2½ to 3 tablespoons fresh lime juice

Salt and pepper to taste

FAST, FRESH, AND FEISTY, this salsa goes great with a big bowl of chips and a sunny afternoon. For a tasty twist, try adding some fresh cilantro, and be sure to save a sprig for garnish. Whatever you do, just be careful to wash your hands after chopping the jalapeño. I learned that one the hard way!

1. Using a sharp knife or food processor, dice or pulse all of the ingredients to an even consistency. Add lime juice and season to taste.

Edamame Hummus

I TOOK THIS RECIPE to the Gig Harbor Gluten-Free Group meeting so the members could be my taste testers. I was surprised at the number of people who really liked this version of hummus. I thought some might not care for the unique taste of edamame, but it was a huge hit. This hummus recipe calls for lemon juice, but I bet it would taste just as good with lime juice. Serve with carrots, celery, apple slices, brown rice chips, crackers, or whatever you prefer.

1. Place the frozen edamame in a saucepan and cover with water. Heat to a boil and then simmer for 3 to 4 minutes, or until tender and then drain and cool.

2. Once the edamame is cool, place the beans in a food processor along with all of the other ingredients (except 1 teaspoon olive oil) and pulse until mixture is very smooth. You don't want lumps in the hummus, so be sure you pulse it long enough. Set the mixture aside or place in the refrigerator for 20 to 30 minutes to allow the flavors to blend. Drizzle on 1teaspoon of olive oil before serving.

MAKES 1½ CUPS

1 (12-ounce) bag of frozen shelled edamame

1 to 2 teaspoons minced garlic (or more to taste)

3 tablespoons plus 1 teaspoon fresh lemon juice

2 tablespoons plus 1 teaspoon organic extra virgin olive oil

¾ teaspoon kosher salt

½ teaspoon cumin

¼ teaspoon dried chipotle pepper

Pinch of cinnamon

Red Pepper Hummus

MAKES 1½ CUPS

1 (15-ounce) can garbanzo
    beans, rinsed and drained

6 tablespoons sesame tahini

½ teaspoon minced garlic

2 to 3 tablespoons olive oil

½ cup chopped piquanté or
    red bell peppers

4 tablespoons lemon juice

1 tablespoon chopped fresh
    cilantro

¼ teaspoon cumin

Pinch of cayenne pepper

Salt and pepper to taste
    (optional)

NO DOUBLE DIPPING! In less than fifteen minutes you've got an amazing spread for sandwiches, a delicious party dip, or a quick and easy snack. Try it with gluten-free chips or your favorite crudités. If you already have presoaked beans in the kitchen, drain them and use about 2 cups to substitute for the canned garbanzos.

1. Using a blender or food processor, purée all ingredients to a smooth consistency, approximately 2 minutes. Transfer to a serving dish and drizzle with olive oil. Add a sprig of cilantro and a pinch of black pepper or cayenne pepper to garnish.

Spinach Dip

SERVE THIS DIP with your favorite crudités—such as carrots, celery, cherry tomatoes, sliced bell peppers—or as another option, use this dip to stuff tomatoes or pickled piquanté peppers. This dip stores well in an airtight container in the refrigerator for several days.

1. In a small saucepan, heat the olive oil over medium-high heat and then add the onion and sauté until soft, about 4 minutes. Add in the garlic and sauté a few minutes longer. Turn off the heat and set aside.

2. Place the steamed, drained spinach and all other ingredients (Tofutti sour cream, lemon juice, ground cashews, onions, garlic, sea salt, and pepper) in a food processor and pulse until they are well blended.

3. Place mixture in serving bowl and season with salt and pepper to taste. Refrigerate before serving.

MAKES ABOUT 2 ½ CUPS

1 tablespoon olive oil
½ cup finely chopped onion
1 to 2 cloves garlic, minced
1 cup packed fresh spinach, steamed and drained
3 tablespoons Tofutti sour cream
1 tablespoon lemon or orange juice
1 cup ground raw cashews, finely ground in a food processor
¼ teaspoon sea salt
Fresh cracked pepper to taste

Stuffed Tomatoes

MAKES 12 STUFFED TOMATOES

2 avocados, diced

1 cup peeled, diced kiwi

2 tablespoons finely chopped red bell pepper

2 tablespoons plus 1 teaspoon fresh lime juice

2 teaspoons maple syrup

2 green onions, finely chopped (save a small amount for garnish)

¼ teaspoon sea salt

1 tablespoon organic sugar (or agave)

Fresh cracked pepper and salt to taste

12 cherry tomatoes, washed

I LOVE AVOCADOS. So any chance I get to use them in a recipe, I take. I like this recipe because it's quick, easy, full of flavor, and great to take to a gathering of friends. You can stuff so many things inside these bite-size morsels. Try the Red Pepper Hummus (page 58), Edamame Hummus (page 57), Mock Egg Salad (page 119), or whatever else your heart desires.

1. Slice, dice, and prepare your vegetables and fruit and then toss everything together (minus the tomatoes) into a large bowl and stir well. Season to taste with salt and pepper.

2. Prepare the cherry tomatoes by cutting off the bottoms of them so they will sit erect on a plate. Scoop out the center with a small spoon or melon scoop and throw the center away. Fill the bite-size tomato with the avocado and kiwi mixture and garnish with finely chopped green onions, if desired.

Best Banana and Chocolate Chip Cookies

THESE COOKIES ARE a child's dream come true. Big kids will love them too! I had more than twenty taste testers for this recipe, and the only comment I heard was "May I have another?" I made these cookies the first time while on Kauai and the apple bananas there are just heavenly. We don't have apple bananas in Washington, but that's OK— these cookies still taste great!

1. Preheat the oven to 350°F. Line a cookie sheet with parchment paper.

2. Begin by soaking the chia seeds in 2 tablespoons warm water for at least 5 to 10 minutes, or until gelatin-like in texture.

3. In a large mixing bowl, blend together vegan buttery spread and coconut palm sugar. Add chia seed mixture and vanilla, stirring well to incorporate. Add mashed banana. Once combined, add dry ingredients, including brown rice flour and sorghum, baking powder and baking soda, cinnamon, and salt. Stir well. Now, mixing by hand, incorporate the chocolate chips and nuts.

4. Drop cookie dough by tablespoon onto the prepared cookie sheet and bake for 13 to 15 minutes, or until golden brown. Cool on a wire rack.

MAKES 14 LARGE COOKIES

- 1 teaspoon chia seeds mixed with 2 tablespoon water
- ¾ cup vegan buttery spread or extra virgin coconut oil
- 1 cup coconut palm sugar or agave nectar
- 1 teaspoon vanilla
- ½ cup mashed banana
- 1 cup brown rice flour
- 1 cup sorghum flour
- 2 teaspoons baking powder
- 1 teaspoon baking soda
- 1 teaspoon cinnamon
- ½ teaspoon salt
- ½ cup chocolate chips (Enjoy Life Foods or other vegan chips)
- ½ cup chopped walnuts (optional)

Candied Nuts

MAKES 3 CUPS

1 cup raw walnuts

1 cup raw pecans

1 cup raw almonds

4 tablespoons organic maple syrup

½ teaspoon cinnamon

THESE ARE GREAT on salads, my favorite being the Spinach Salad on page 123. You can also serve these as a snack, which I often do at family gatherings, or give them as a gift, packaged in a lovely jar with a ribbon during the holidays. The nuts can be chopped if desired or left whole.

1. Preheat oven to 300°F.

2. Place all the nuts in a bowl and drizzle with the maple syrup and cinnamon. Stir well to mix together.

3. Spread the nut mixture out on a baking sheet (with edges) and slowly toast in the oven, stirring 2 to 3 times during the baking process, until the nuts are toasted, about 20 minutes.

4. Cool and store in an airtight container.

Chocolate Power Balls

LIKE CHOCOLATE? Like a quick power boost without caffeine? This is the recipe for you! Take these to work, send them off to school with the kids, take them on a hike or to the beach—the list is endless. If you are allergic to nuts, make this with seeds. Replace the cashews and walnuts with sunflower seeds, pumpkin seeds, sesame seeds, or flaxseeds. Consider adding dried cherries or cranberries. My taste testers loved these, and I am quite sure you will too! These store in the fridge for up to one week.

1. Place the nuts and dates in a food processor and pulse until ground. Add the rest of the ingredients and whirl until the mixture begins to form a ball.

2. Remove the mixture from the food processor and put in a large bowl. Spread some waxed paper on a cookie sheet and with clean hands, form small balls (about tablespoon-size) and place them on the cookie sheet. Place in the refrigerator for about an hour to harden.

MAKES ABOUT 16 BALLS

1 cup walnuts

1 cup cashews

1 cup pitted and chopped Medjool dates

1 tablespoon chia seeds

1 tablespoon pure vanilla

½ cup Enjoy Life Foods vegan chocolate chips

½ teaspoon cinnamon

⅛ to ¼ teaspoon cardamom

1 tablespoon water or orange juice

Peanut Butter–Chocolate Chip Fudge

1 cup vegan margarine

1 cup peanut butter (creamy or crunchy, both work well)

1 teaspoon vanilla

2 tablespoons organic maple syrup

4 cups powdered sugar

½ cup vegan chocolate chips

MY GRANDMA used to make peanut butter fudge during the holidays, so I thought I would try to make a modern version. I had no idea it would be such a big hit! Be careful—it is addicting! It does have sugar in it, so if you are sugar-free, best to avoid this one.

1. Line an 8 x 8-inch square pan with wax paper.

2. Melt the margarine and peanut butter in a medium-size heavy pot. When the butters are melted, turn off the heat and add the vanilla and maple syrup and stir well.

3. Slowly beat in the powdered sugar (with a wooden spoon) until the sugar is completely blended. Add in the chocolate chips and stir with a wooden spoon. Don't over mix the chocolate chips, they should swirl throughout the peanut butter fudge.

4. Immediately spread the mixture into the prepared pan. Spread with clean fingers, until the mixture is evenly spread in the pan. Refrigerate until cool.

Kids' Favorites

Grilled Cheese Sandwiches

GRILLED CHEESE sandwiches can be boring on their own, but add some grilled onions and avocado and you have a whole new twist on the traditional sandwich. You can also add Dijon mustard, fresh sprouts, or sliced tomatoes to make it a hearty meal! Serve with a salad, fruit, or chips.

1. Lightly spread some olive oil spread (such as Earth Balance Buttery Spread) on both sides of each piece of bread. On one side of the bread, spread 1 tablespoon of the cheese. Top the cheese with the avocado and onions (sprouts, too, if desired) and then sandwich the two breads together. Do this for both sandwiches.

2. Heat a skillet to medium heat and then add a small amount of olive oil spread (½ tablespoon) and let it heat up. When it is hot, add the sandwiches and grill until done on both sides. About 2 to 3 minutes on each side should do it.

SERVES 2

½ to 1 tablespoon olive oil spread

4 slices of Millet Bread (see page 101 for recipe)

2 tablespoons hickory-flavored WayFare vegan cheese or Daiya Deliciously Dairy Free Cheddar Style Shreds (they are delicious!)

1 cup grilled or sautéed onions (sauté onions in a small saucepan over medium-high heat, in 1 tablespoon olive oil until soft and lightly browned)

½ avocado, pitted and sliced thin

Sprouts, tomatoes, or other garnishes

Fried "Chicken" Nuggets

**MAKES
APPROXIMATELY
20 NUGGETS**

1 (8-ounce) package of
gluten-free tempeh, cut
into ½-inch cubes

1 tablespoon vegan chicken
broth powder (or bouillon
cubes)

½ cup hot water

⅔ cup crushed gluten-free
cornflakes

1 tablespoon sorghum flour

½ teaspoon organic natural
sea salt (I use Redmond
Organic Seasoning Salt)

¼ to ½ teaspoon freshly
ground black pepper

1 tablespoon baking powder

1 tablespoon nutritional
yeast, more if desired

½ cup potato flour

½ cup grapeseed oil

THESE NUGGETS are made from tempeh, and while they don't taste exactly like traditional chicken nuggets, they come close. An alternative to frying would be to bake them. If you can't find vegan chicken broth powder, just increase the nutritional yeast to 2 to 3 tablespoons.

1. Cut the tempeh into cubes and place in a bowl with the vegan chicken powder or bouillon cubes. Pour the hot water over the tempeh mixture and stir to coat well. Let rest for 15 to 30 minutes.

2. In a mixing bowl, combine the crushed cornflakes, sorghum flour, salt, pepper, baking powder, yeast, and potato flour. Stir to fully mix ingredients. Remove the tempeh from the soaking liquid, but do not discard the liquid. Dip the tempeh into the crushed cornflake mixture, then dip it back into the soaking liquid and repeat. Press the cornflake mixture into the tempeh, so that it is well coated. Each cube of tempeh should now be double dipped.

3. In a large skillet, heat ¼ cup of the grapeseed oil to medium-high heat, then add about half of the coated tempeh. The nuggets will cook very quickly, so be sure to watch them closely. As soon as they are brown, flip them over until all of the sides are evenly cooked, about 4 to 5 minutes. Remove from pan and drain on a paper towel. After the first batch is done, discard the oil, clean the skillet, and reheat with the remaining ¼ cup of oil. Repeat the process.

4. Serve plain or with a Ranch-style dressing.

Mac and Cheese

SEVERAL OF MY FRIENDS laughed when I told them I was developing a gluten-free, vegan mac and cheese recipe. They said, "You can't make a dish that tastes like 'regular' mac and cheese." But I said, "Oh, yeah?" Well, here it is. And I swear that when I served this to my movie night group, I saw at least one person licking her dish! Since I developed this recipe, I have found a new "mock cheddar cheese" that is made from oatmeal, not soy. It's called WayFare Hickory-Smoked Cheddar-Style Spread. It would be good in this recipe if you want to replace the soy cheese. Be adventurous, give it a go! Another vegan cheese that you can use in this recipe is called Daiya. It comes in Cheddar flavor or Pepper Jack. Made from a pea protein, it melts and stretches very well.

1. Preheat oven to 350°F.

2. Heat a large skillet over medium-high heat and add the oil. When the oil is hot, add the onion and sauté until it is translucent and soft, about 4 minutes. Add in the arrowroot and stir until well blended, then immediately add in 1 cup of the milk and whisk the mixture until it begins to thicken. Keep whisking the mixture and add in another cup of the milk and the Dijon mustard, and then reduce the heat to medium.

(continues)

SERVES 4 TO 6

1 tablespoon olive oil

1 cup finely chopped onion

1 tablespoon arrowroot

2 cups coconut milk (So Delicious, or other milk of your liking), divided

1 tablespoon Dijon mustard

½ cup Tofutti sour cream

3 cups grated Follow Your Heart Vegan Gourmet nacho cheese alternative

½ teaspoon kosher salt or sea salt

¼ teaspoon cumin (if desired)

Lots of fresh cracked pepper to taste (at least ¼ teaspoon)

4 cups dried, gluten-free pasta (Cook according to package directions, then drain. Do not cook pasta until the sauce is nearly finished, so your noodles are hot but not gummy.)

1 tablespoon Earth Balance Natural Buttery Spread or other vegan margarine or coconut oil

⅓ cup crushed brown rice crackers

Mac and Cheese *(continued)*

3. Continue to cook for 2 to 3 minutes, then reduce the heat and add in the sour cream and vegan cheese. Stir mixture well, and then add in the salt, cumin, and lots of fresh cracked pepper.

4. Toss this mixture with the cooked noodles and then pour into a baking dish (9-inch square pan).

5. Heat a small saucepan over medium-high heat and add the tablespoon of margarine. When hot, add the crushed crackers and stir for 1 to 2 minutes, until lightly browned. Top the baking dish with the toasted rice crackers.

6. Bake for about 30 minutes, or until mixture is bubbly and lightly browned on top. The leftovers, if any, can be stored in an airtight container for up to 3 to 4 days.

Mock Chicken Noodle Soup

I HAVE NEVER LIKED traditional chicken soup. I found the diced carrots to be boring, and the chicken flavorless, so I made my version much tastier. I have added lots of vegetables, and instead of chicken, I use cremini mushrooms. This soup is thick, so if you prefer a thinner version, add more vegetable broth. One of my recipe testers didn't have broccoli when she tried this recipe. She is a very creative cook, so she just used the veggies she had in the house and said the flavors were wonderful. So, be creative and don't be afraid to add to this soup. This recipe takes about one and a half hours from start to finish.

1. Heat a Dutch oven or large stockpot over medium-high heat and add the oil. When it is hot, add the onion and cook until it begins to soften, about 4 minutes. Add in the carrots and broccoli and continue to cook 10 minutes more.

2. Add in the celery, roasted peppers, garlic, and mushrooms and stir. Sauté for another 5 minutes and then add the white wine. While that is simmering, in a separate bowl combine the vegan chicken broth powder, herbes de Provence, and nutritional yeast with 2 cups of warm water and whisk together well. Pour into the stockpot and stir.

3. Add in the vegetable broth and 2 cups water as well as the noodles and simmer over medium heat, covered, until the noodles are al dente, about 10 to 20 minutes. Stir the soup frequently, so the noodles

SERVES 8

1 tablespoon olive oil
1 large onion, chopped (2 cups)
3 carrots (2 cups sliced)
2 cups chopped broccoli
¾ cup chopped celery
1 cup chopped roasted red and yellow bell peppers (or just red is fine)
2 to 3 cloves garlic, minced (about 1 tablespoon)
2 cups sliced mushrooms (cremini or other)
⅓ to ½ cup white wine
2 tablespoons vegan chicken broth powder
1 to 2 teaspoons herbes de Provence
2 to 3 tablespoons nutritional yeast
4 cups water
4 cups vegetable broth
6 ounces uncooked brown rice noodles
¼ to ½ teaspoon coarse kosher salt

(continues)

Mock Chicken Noodle Soup *(continued)*

½ teaspoon fresh cracked
  pepper

½ teaspoon red pepper
  (optional)

½ teaspoon chives (optional)

½ cup chopped fresh parsley

do not stick to the bottom of the stockpot. If the soup is simmering too high, turn it down slightly, so the noodles cook, but do not turn to mush!

4. Season to taste with the salt and pepper. I like lots of fresh cracked pepper. Feel free to adjust the herbes de Provence if you wish a stronger flavor. You can also add chives if you like, or other herbs and spices to your liking. Once the noodles are cooked and the vegetables tender, turn the soup off. Garnish with fresh parsley and serve hot.

Note: If you prefer, pre-cook the noodles according to package directions, drain, and then add to the soup. It shortens the cooking time.

Pizza

THIS PIZZA IS QUICK to make, and the toppings provided are just a few that you can use. You might also consider Kalamata olives, capers, spinach, pine nuts, or arugula. Let the kids make the pizza on their own. Their creativity may just knock your taste buds out of the park!

1. Mix all of the sauce ingredients together in a medium-size bowl and set aside for about 15 minutes to allow the flavors to blend.

2. Preheat the oven to 400°F. In a large skillet, heat the oil over medium-high heat and add the onion. Sauté until soft and lightly browned, about 5 to 8 minutes. Add the red bell peppers, sun-dried tomatoes, artichoke hearts, garlic, and mushrooms and sauté an additional minute or two.

3. Spoon the sauce over the pizza crust and then layer the vegetables on top. If desired, top with vegan mozzarella cheese or fresh parsley and sliced tomato. Bake for about 20 to 30 minutes, or until crust is done and topping (if using cheese) is bubbly.

SERVES 6 TO 8

1 premade Pizza Crust
   (see recipe on page 74)

Sauce
1 (6-ounce) can tomato paste
½ cup water
2 tablespoons chopped fresh
   parsley
1 tablespoon chopped fresh
   tarragon
1 teaspoon dried oregano
2 tablespoons chopped fresh
   basil (optional)
½ teaspoon kosher sea salt
Fresh cracked pepper to taste

Toppings
1 to 2 teaspoons olive oil
½ to ¾ cup sliced onion
½ cup sliced roasted red bell
   pepper
¼ cup chopped sun-dried
   tomatoes
½ cup sliced artichoke hearts
   (optional)
3 or 4 cloves garlic, peeled
   and minced
½ cup sliced mushrooms
Fresh parsley for garnish
1 cup grated rice mozzarella
   cheese (optional)
1 large tomato, sliced
   (optional)

Pizza Crust

2¼ teaspoons baking yeast

1¼ cups water (warm, 110°F
to 115°F)

2 teaspoons organic palm
sugar

2 cups tapioca flour

1 cup sorghum flour

½ cup coconut flour

½ cup millet flour

3 teaspoons baking powder

1 teaspoon sea salt

2 teaspoons guar gum

4 tablespoons warm water

2 teaspoons chia seeds

¼ cup organic extra virgin
olive oil

½ teaspoon Bragg's apple
cider vinegar

THIS PIZZA CRUST recipe makes two small (10-inch to 12-inch) pizzas, or one large pizza. I like it because it is easy to make, and the flavor will not overpower the toppings you add. If you don't have coconut flour it's no big deal; you can replace it with either more sorghum or millet flour or a half cup of rice flour. I think everyone will like this recipe! It takes about forty-five minutes, tops, to prepare.

1. Place the yeast in a large bowl and add ½ cup of the warm water and the sugar. Let this mixture sit for about 10 to 15 minutes, or until bubbly (proofed).

2. While the yeast is activating, combine all of the flours, baking powder, salt, and guar gum in a medium-size bowl and stir to mix together well. Set aside.

3. In a small bowl, combine the 4 tablespoons of warm water with the chia seeds and whisk this mixture together for a minute and then let it sit for 5 to 10 minutes, or until it thickens.

4. In a medium bowl, combine the rest of the warm water (¾ cup), the olive oil, and the cider vinegar and stir well to incorporate.

5. When the yeast is activated, add in 1 cup of the flour mixture and stir well to incorporate. Then, alternate with the rest of the ingredients, adding in the chia seed mixture; then some of the flour mixture; the water, oil, and vinegar mixture; and so on, until you have incorporated all of the ingredients together. Mix the dough together well, until it is nice and smooth.

6. If you want two pizzas you can divide your dough. I use a large pizza stone, and I use all of the dough for one pizza. So, the next step is to press the pizza dough onto your pizza pan(s) or pizza stone. The dough can be sticky, so I wet my hands slightly and press the dough out until it fills the pizza stone. Depending on how thick or thin you like your pizza crust, you can adjust to your own preferences.

7. Set the pizza crust in a warm place (I heat my oven to 200°F, then shut it off, open the door, and put the pizza crust inside) for about 15 minutes.

8. Preheat your oven to 400°F and bake the pizza crust until lightly browned, about 10 to 15 minutes.

9. If you wish, you can use the pizza sauce found on page 73 (canned sauce works, too), then add your favorite precooked veggies and broil for 4 to 5 minutes. You can also bake this pizza crust again, with the toppings on it, but I find that it is easier just to sauté some veggies while the crust is baking and then throw them on top with some fresh basil and other herbs, and then broil to melt the (vegan) cheese. I don't often use cheese, but I broil the pizza, complete with toppings for about 8 minutes to heat it through and brown the crust.

Roasted Yam Home Fries

**SERVES 2 TO 4 AS
A SIDE DISH**

2 tablespoons coconut oil
4 cups peeled, cubed red
    garnet yams, cut into
    1-inch cubes
Kosher salt and fresh ground
    pepper to taste
Nutmeg to taste

I LOVE FRENCH FRIES. I know they are not good for us, so I decided years ago to make my own version of them, using red garnet yams. (These are actually sweet potatoes, as we don't really have true yams in the United States). Anyway, in this version, organic coconut oil provides a lovely flavor and crunchiness to the potatoes.

1. Preheat the oven to 400°F.

2. Melt the coconut oil in a cast-iron skillet or heavy saucepan and then add in the yams. Stir until the yams are coated in oil.

3. Lightly salt and pepper the yams and place them in the oven. Roast, stirring frequently for about 40 minutes, or until they are crunchy on the outside and fork tender on the inside. Season with fresh grated nutmeg and if desired, additional salt and pepper. You can also season these fries with fresh rosemary, herbes de Provence, or Spike seasonings.

Note: You can also bake these on a cookie sheet, if you prefer.

Chocolate Cupcakes

CHOCOLATE doesn't have to contain dairy to wow your taste buds! There are several vegan cocoas and chocolate chips on the market that are really good. If you want to dress these cupcakes up for a party, top them with either the Cashew Butter or Peanut Butter Frosting (page 202) or the Orange Icing (page 205).

1. Preheat the oven to 350°F. Grease a muffin pan with canola oil.

2. In a small bowl, combine the ¾ cup milk and the apple cider vinegar. Set aside.

3. In a large mixing bowl, beat together the short-ening, sugar, and brown sugar until well blended. In a small bowl, whisk together the egg replacer and 4 tablespoons of milk. You really need to whisk this well until the mixture becomes bubbly. Then add the egg replacer, applesauce, and vanilla to the shortening-sugar mixture and mix for a few minutes to combine fully.

4. In a separate large bowl, combine all of the flours, cocoa powder, baking powder, baking soda, sea salt, and guar gum.

5. Alternate mixing the dry ingredients in with the wet ones. Add a small amount of the flour mixture to the mixing bowl with the shortening-sugar mixture. Add in a small amount of the milk and cider

(continues)

MAKES 10 TO 12 CUPCAKES

¾ cup soy, hemp, coconut, or rice milk (I use So Delicious coconut milk)

¾ teaspoon apple cider vinegar

¼ cup palm shortening or vegan margarine

½ cup organic sugar

¼ cup organic brown sugar

3 teaspoons Ener-G egg replacer

4 tablespoons So Delicious coconut milk

2 tablespoons applesauce

1 teaspoon vanilla

¼ cup coconut flour

½ cup sorghum flour

½ cup brown rice flour

¼ cup cocoa powder

1 teaspoon baking powder

½ teaspoon baking soda

½ teaspoon sea salt

½ teaspoon guar gum or xanthan gum

Peanut butter frosting (page 202)

Chocolate Cupcakes (continued)

mixture you set aside earlier, then more of the flour, then milk, etc., until you have incorporated both the milk and the dry ingredients into the wet. Stir to mix well.

6. Pour the batter into the prepared muffin pan, filling each cup halfway. Bake for 16 to 18 minutes or until a toothpick comes out clean. Cool on a wire rack.

7. Frost the cupcakes with the Peanut Butter Frosting or any frosting of your choosing.

Chocolate Tapioca Pudding

I DON'T KNOW ABOUT YOU, but I think of tapioca pudding as total comfort food. Tapioca pudding is not commonly made with chocolate, but I love to try different things, so I thought I would add it to this recipe. You could get very adventurous and add in a dash of chipotle pepper or cinnamon or top it with some chopped macadamia nuts or fresh peaches. I like my tapioca pudding served warm, so if you prefer that too, just get yourself a bowl before you put it in the refrigerator.

The pudding takes about twenty minutes to make, but there is time on both sides for setting in the fridge, so total time is about two and a half hours.

1. In a small bowl, combine the tapioca and 1 cup of the milk. Place it in the refrigerator for 1 hour.

2. Melt the chocolate chips in a double boiler set over boiling water. When the tapioca has set for an hour, remove the chocolate from the double boiler, pour the water out of the bottom saucepan, and then scrape the chocolate into the saucepan, along with the tapioca and milk mixture.

3. Add in the maple syrup, agave, additional cup of milk, and pinch of salt and heat to boiling. When the mixture reaches the boiling point, add in the arrowroot and whisk until well blended. Continue to cook over high heat until the mixture begins to boil again, and it thickens. Turn off the heat once the tapioca mixture is thick and add the vanilla, stirring to incorporate. Pour into 4 ramekins, or a bowl if you prefer, and place in the refrigerator for 1 hour.

SERVES 4

⅓ cup tapioca pearls (not instant)
2 cups So Delicious coconut milk, divided
½ cup Enjoy Life Foods vegan chocolate chips
¼ cup maple syrup
¼ cup agave cactus nectar
Pinch of salt
1 tablespoon arrowroot
1½ teaspoons vanilla

Coconut, Blueberry, and Banana Milkshake

SERVES 1

1 cup Coconut Bliss nondairy
   ice cream
1 banana, mashed
1 cup blueberries
½ teaspoon vanilla extract
½ to 1 cup nondairy milk
   (soy, rice, hemp, nut, or
   coconut)
Pinch of cinnamon (optional)

THE KIDS WILL LOVE THIS! Serve chilled in a tall, slender glass, with a few fresh berries for garnish. Add a curly straw for full effect, and even the grown-ups won't be able to resist!

1. Toss everything into the blender, and blend on high. If the consistency is too thick, just add more milk. You can always add more fruit if you like too, which will make the recipe into more of a smoothie. Try peach-banana, strawberry-banana, or just go plain bananas!

Peanut Butter–Chocolate Chip Rice Crispy Dessert

THIS RECIPE WAS A HUGE HIT with all of my neighbors, especially the kids. They kept asking me for seconds and thirds, so I know it will dazzle your loved ones as well. I heard one of the boys asking his mom as they walked away if she would make him some more!

1. Mix all of the ingredients together in a large bowl. You are going to need some muscle to stir this together well. If you want, wash your hands and mix the ingredients together that way!

2. Grease a square 8 x 8-inch or 9 x 9-inch pan (depending on what size you have available) with canola oil and then press the mixture evenly into the pan. Refrigerator for an hour or so and then cut into bars.

MAKES ABOUT 20 TO 24 BARS

- 4 cups gluten-free, crispy rice cereal
- 1 cup peanut butter (or almond, cashew, or sunflower seed butter)
- 1 teaspoon vanilla
- ½ cup chopped walnuts (or other nuts or seeds)
- ½ cup vegan chocolate chips
- 1 to 2 tablespoons brown rice syrup or sorghum syrup

Peach and Blueberry Cobbler

SERVES 4 TO 6

Fruit

4 to 5 cups sliced peaches

1½ cups fresh organic
    blueberries or
      1 (10-ounce) bag frozen
    blueberries

Batter

¼ cup tapioca flour

¼ cup coconut flour

½ cup all-purpose gluten-
    free flour (substitute
    sorghum if you prefer)

¼ cup brown rice flour

1 teaspoon baking powder

½ teaspoon sea salt

1 teaspoon cinnamon

¼ cup coconut palm sugar

¼ cup vegan margarine

¾ cup So Delicious coconut
    milk

Topping

½ cup oats

¼ cup organic palm sugar

½ teaspoon cinnamon

½ cup sorghum flour

½ cup chopped pecans

PETER RABBIT'S Blueberry Coffee Cake was my son Rory's favorite as a child. The recipe in his Beatrix Potter cookbook has all the stains to prove it! Inspired by the original, this cobbler is sure to be a hit with the kids. You could also dress it up with a garnish and a glass of Champagne, and I bet the grown-up kids will love it too!

1. Preheat the oven to 350°F.

2. Grease a 9 x 9-inch baking dish with canola oil and arrange the fruit evenly in the bottom of the dish.

3. To prepare the batter, combine the dry ingredients, including the sugar, in a large mixing bowl. Cut in the margarine, and then stir in the milk with a wooden spoon. Spread the batter evenly over the fruit. You may have to use your hands to carefully do this.

4. In a small bowl, combine the topping ingredients until well mixed, then sprinkle over the cobbler. Bake for 45 to 50 minutes, or until golden brown.

Pumpkin Cupcakes

KIDS LOVE THESE CUPCAKES! You do not need to frost them as they are great on their own, but the Orange Icing (page 205) does add a nice burst of flavor. If you prefer less fat, use ¼ cup of canola oil and ½ cup of applesauce. You won't notice much change in the texture of the cupcakes, but it will reduce the fat considerably.

1. Preheat the oven to 350°F. Grease a muffin pan with canola oil.

2. In a large bowl, combine the oil and sugar together until well blended. Add in the egg replacer and applesauce and keep mixing until well incorporated. Add in the pumpkin and coconut milk and stir together until mixed well.

3. In a separate bowl, combine the flours, baking powder, and baking soda, sea salt, guar gum, and cinnamon. Stir together really well and then add the dry ingredients to the wet ingredients until they are incorporated. Spoon mixture into the prepared muffin pan, filling each cup halfway with the pumpkin mixture.

4. Bake for 20 to 25 minutes. The cupcakes will be done when a toothpick inserted into the middle of one comes out clean; test at 20 minutes for doneness. Cool on a wire rack.

MAKES 12 CUPCAKES

½ cup canola oil

¼ cup organic sugar or palm sugar

1½ teaspoons Ener-G egg replacer (whisked together really well with 2 tablespoons warm water, mixing until bubbly)

¼ cup applesauce, unsweetened

1 cup cooked pumpkin (canned is okay)

½ cup So Delicious coconut milk (or soy milk if you prefer)

1 ½ cups sorghum flour

½ cup brown rice flour

3 teaspoons baking powder

½ teaspoon baking soda

½ teaspoon sea salt

½ teaspoon guar gum or xanthan gum

1½ teaspoons cinnamon

All-American Sides

Baked Beans

AN O'BRIEN FAMILY gathering without baked beans is like the Fourth of July without fireworks. From picnics to barbeques, at the park or at the beach, this side dish goes with everything. So put on your apron, fire up the grill, and give me some o' those beans! By the way, if you can't find Cajun seasoning at the grocery store, you can make your own with a dash each of the following: paprika, onion, garlic powder, black pepper, lemon peel, chili powder, allspice, cloves, thyme, mace, red pepper flakes, and bay leaf.

1. In a large skillet, sauté the onion in the olive oil over medium-high heat approximately 3 to 4 minutes, or until soft. Add garlic and sauté another 1 to 2 minutes. Add the beans and reduce heat to medium-low, stirring to combine ingredients.

2. Add the remaining ingredients, season to taste, and allow to simmer over low heat until the flavors have combined and desired consistency is achieved, approximately 15 minutes, stirring occasionally.

SERVES 4

¼ cup finely chopped onion

½ tablespoon olive oil

⅛ teaspoon crushed garlic (optional)

3 cups organic canned white kidney beans, drained and rinsed

½ cup ketchup

3 tablespoons maple syrup

2 tablespoons brown sugar

1 tablespoon blackstrap molasses

½ teaspoon Tabasco sauce

½ teaspoon freshly ground black pepper

½ teaspoon Cajun Creole seasoning

Garlic Mashed Potatoes

SERVES 4

1 head garlic, peeled

1 to 2 tablespoons olive oil, divided

6 or 7 potatoes

½ cup coconut or soy creamer, plain

Vegetable broth (optional)

Vegan margarine

Salt and pepper

SO SIMPLE AND SO DELICIOUS! For a bit of color and texture, I prefer red potatoes with the skins left on, but you can use whatever potatoes you wish. If you want to add gravy, I would leave out the garlic, and use my Mushroom Gravy with Red Wine on page 91. In any case, be sure to make enough for a second helping!

1. Preheat the oven to 400°F.

2. Place the garlic in aluminum foil, drizzle with olive oil, tightly seal, and bake 25 to 30 minutes.

3. While the garlic is roasting, cook the potatoes.

4. When garlic is cool to the touch, squeeze out the individual cloves into a bowl. Mash together with the drained potatoes. Add the creamer and olive oil, and if potatoes are still too dry, add vegetable broth until desired consistency is achieved. Add vegan margarine and salt and pepper to taste.

Green Bean Casserole

TRADITIONAL OR NOT, I never did care for the canned mushroom soup and shoestring green beans typically used in this beloved recipe. But the fresh mushroom sauce in this version tastes great. If soy bothers you, try using Creamy Cashew Milk or coconut creamer (see page 206) in place of the Tofutti sour cream. And if you like your casserole really saucy, double the amount of broth and sour cream.

1. Preheat the oven to 350°F.

2. On the stovetop, heat a large skillet to medium-high and add the olive oil. When it is hot, add the onions and cook until soft, about 4 minutes. Add in the mushrooms and continue to cook over medium heat until the mushrooms begin to release their juices, about 4 to 5 minutes. Add in the vegetable broth and sour cream and season with salt and pepper. Turn off the heat.

3. Place the green beans in either a steamer, or a double boiler set over boiling water. Steaming takes 4 to 5 minutes. Once the beans are crisply tender, place them in a quart-size casserole dish and pour the sauce over the top. Stir to mix the sauce with the beans and then, if desired, spread grated nondairy cheese over the top.

4. Heat a small skillet to medium-high heat and add the cracker crumbs when hot. Stir around to lightly brown, then sprinkle over the top of the green bean casserole and bake for about 20 minutes, or until bubbly.

SERVES 4

1 tablespoon olive oil
½ cup finely chopped onion
1 cup cleaned and sliced
    mushrooms
½ cup vegetable broth
½ cup Tofutti sour cream
Salt and pepper to taste
3 cups chopped green
    beans, ½-inch or 1-inch
    pieces
1 cup grated rice or soy
    cheddar cheese (optional;
    Follow Your Heart Vegan
    Gourmet nacho cheese
    alternative really adds
    flavor to this dish)
¼ cup crushed cracker
    crumbs (or brown rice
    chips)

Mashed Sweet Potatoes (Yams)

SERVES 4

3 garnet yams, peeled and quartered

2 tablespoons orange juice, fresh squeezed if possible

3 to 4 tablespoons organic vegetable broth

¼ cup cleaned, chopped leeks, white part only

2 cloves garlic, peeled and minced

1 to 2 tablespoons white wine (with fruity flavors—pear, apple, melon—such as a Chardonnay)

Pinch of nutmeg, fresh grated, if possible (optional)

Pinch of cardamom (optional)

¼ teaspoon sea salt

Fresh cracked pepper to taste

THIS RECIPE IS GREAT served with the Mushroom Gravy (page 91) on top, or by itself, served along with the grilled Portobello Mushroom Steaks (page 140). If you are really adventurous, you can serve this as the topping for the Vegetable Pot-pie (page 145). I do not use white sweet potatoes in this recipe; I like the orange color of the garnet yams.

1. In a stockpot, cover the yams with water and heat to boiling. Cook until the yams are fork tender. Remove from heat and drain. Set aside.

2. In a medium-size saucepan, heat the orange juice and vegetable broth until hot. Add the leeks and sauté until soft, about 5 minutes. Add in the garlic and, stirring frequently, sauté another 1 to 2 minutes. Add the yams and mash together with the leeks and garlic. Add the wine and stir to incorporate. Add the nutmeg, cardamom, salt, and pepper and cook over low heat, stirring frequently, until flavors are blended. Add more vegetable broth, if needed, to ensure yams are fluffy and do not stick to the pan.

Mushroom Gravy with Red Wine

THIS GRAVY IS DELICIOUS served over mashed potatoes, but it can also be served over noodles, vegetables, or even biscuits. The red wine adds a lovely color and flavor and the mushrooms provide a hearty base.

1. Heat a large skillet over medium-high heat and add 1 tablespoon olive oil. When hot, add the onion and sauté until soft, about 4 minutes. Add the mushrooms and 2 tablespoons vegetable broth and sauté until the mushrooms are soft and they begin to release their juices, about 5 minutes. Remove from the heat and place this mixture in a bowl. Set aside.

2. Heat the skillet to medium heat and add 2 tablespoons olive oil and ½ cup brown rice flour. Whisk together to mix well; keep whisking and slowly add the remaining 1 cup vegetable broth and the coconut milk–canola oil mixture, whisking constantly. Once the mixture is fully incorporated and begins to thicken add ¼ cup red wine and the onion-mushroom mixture and reduce the heat to medium-low. Cook for 15 to 20 minutes. Add salt and lemon pepper to taste and nutmeg if desired. Serve over mashed potatoes or biscuits. If mixture is too thick, add a bit more vegetable broth until you reach desired consistency.

MAKES ABOUT 4 CUPS

3 tablespoons olive oil, divided

¾ cup finely chopped onion

5 cups sliced mushrooms (cremini or other)

1 cup plus 2 tablespoons vegetable broth

½ cup brown rice flour

1½ cups coconut milk mixed with ¼ cup canola oil

¼ cup red wine (Cabernet works well in this recipe)

Salt to taste

½ teaspoon lemon pepper

Pinch of nutmeg (optional)

Roasted Brussels Sprouts

SERVES 4

2 pounds Brussels sprouts

2 tablespoons organic extra virgin olive oil

2 tablespoons maple syrup

1 tablespoon fresh-squeezed orange juice

1 teaspoon minced garlic (optional)

1 teaspoon herbes de Provence

Salt and pepper to taste

I LOVE POPCORN at the movies . . . but I also love Brussels sprouts. If you haven't tried making a tub of extra salty sprouts and sneaking them into the theater, this recipe will change your life! Done right, these hearty little vegetables can be the perfect finger food, a handsome side dish, or a healthy snack even the kids will love.

1. Preheat the oven to 400°F.

2. Remove any tough or unsightly outer leaves from the Brussels sprouts, cut off the bottom of the stems, and wash thoroughly. When using large sprouts, cut in half to reduce cooking time.

3. Place the Brussels sprouts in a 9 x 13-inch baking dish, and drizzle with olive oil, maple syrup, and orange juice. Add garlic and herbes de Provence, and season with salt and pepper to taste. Mix well to thoroughly coat sprouts. Depending on the size of the sprouts, cooking time will vary. Bake for approximately 30 to 40 minutes. Stir every 10 to 15 minutes to ensure an even roast. Poke the Brussels sprouts with a fork to test for doneness. Do not let them overcook and turn to mush!

Roasted Beets

I MAY HAVE MENTIONED in my previous vegan cookbook that I never liked beets as a child, but I love them now! I absolutely adore them roasted, served as a side dish, in a risotto like the one found on page 143, in stews, or in salads.

2 pounds fresh beets
1 ½ to 2 tablespoons olive oil
Salt and pepper

1. Preheat the oven to 400°F.

2. Wash, peel, and slice the beets into ½- to 1-inch-thick wedges. Drizzle with olive oil and season with salt and pepper.

3. Using aluminum foil, create a roasting pouch for the beets by placing them in the center and tightly sealing the foil around them. Roast for 60 to 65 minutes, or until tender.

Summer Spaghetti Sauce

SERVES 4

2 tablespoons olive oil

1 large yellow onion, approximately 2 cups chopped

1 large leek, white part only, approximately ½ cup chopped (optional)

1 cup chopped green beans

1 cup chopped zucchini

3 cups chopped fresh spinach

6 to 10 pitted and chopped Kalamata olives

1 cup cleaned and chopped cremini mushrooms

3 to 4 cloves garlic, chopped

1 (14.5-ounce) can organic diced tomatoes

1 (28-ounce) can organic tomato sauce

1 cup adzuki or cannellini beans, drained and rinsed

1 heaping tablespoon dried oregano

2 or 3 bay leaves

¼ cup chopped fresh basil

¼ to ½ cup red wine or vegetable broth

½ teaspoon each of salt and pepper, or to taste

HEALTHY, HEARTY, and homemade! This sauce is all about fresh ingredients and good timing. Because different ingredients require different cooking times, it is important to follow the sequence below, so that the rich flavors have a chance to combine. Try this on your favorite gluten-free pasta, or think outside the box and put it on Bruschetta (page 53) or use it as a sauce for Pizza (page 73).

1. In a large saucepan or Dutch oven, heat the olive oil to medium-high. Sauté the onions approximately 4 minutes, or until translucent.

2. Add leeks, green beans, and zucchini and cook another 5 minutes. Then add the spinach and Kalamata olives and continue cooking another 5 minutes before adding the mushrooms. (Stir ingredients as you add them to ensure even cooking.)

3. Allow the vegetables and mushrooms to cook an additional 3 to 4 minutes, then add the garlic and cook for another minute. Finally, stir in the diced tomatoes, tomato sauce, cannellini beans, herbs, spices, red wine or vegetable broth, and salt and pepper.

4. Reduce heat and allow to simmer. Continue cooking until all the flavors have combined and the desired consistency is achieved, about 30 to 45 minutes. Remove bay leaves before serving.

Scalloped Potatoes

WHEN I WAS growing up my grandma Baba made the best scalloped potatoes on the planet. Of course they were made with canned cream of mushroom soup, cheddar cheese, and whole milk. My version is slightly different, but like my grandma's recipe, it is delicious and infused with love. Enjoy! This recipe takes about one and a half hours to prepare.

1. Preheat the oven to 350°F.

2. In a large skillet, heat the oil over medium-high heat and add the onion. Sauté the onion until translucent, about 4 to 5 minutes. Add in the sliced mushrooms and continue to cook until the mushrooms begin to lose their juices and are soft, about 2 to 3 minutes. Add in the sour cream, wine, milk, garlic, herbs, and cinnamon. Whisk until the sour cream is well blended. Do not let the mixture boil. Reduce the heat and add the vegan cheddar cheese. Stir the cheese mixture over medium-low heat until the cheese melts.

3. Place the sliced potatoes in a square 9 x 9-inch baking dish and pour the cheese mixture over the top. Bake for about 45 minutes, or until bubbly.

SERVES 6 TO 8

1 tablespoon organic extra virgin olive oil

1 cup finely chopped onion

1 cup cleaned and sliced mushrooms, stems removed

1 cup vegan sour cream

¼ cup red wine (optional; Cabernet is good in this dish)

½ cup So Delicious coconut milk

½ teaspoon minced garlic

½ teaspoon dried dill

1 teaspoon herbes de Provence

Pinch of cinnamon

2 cups vegan cheddar cheese

6 medium-size new potatoes (4 to 5 cups sliced)

Sweet Potato Gratin

SERVES 6 TO 8

1 to 2 tablespoons olive or
  grapeseed oil
2 pounds sweet potatoes or
  yams, cut into thin slices
2 to 3 Granny Smith apples
  or other tart apple, sliced
  thinly
1 cup orange juice, fresh
  squeezed if possible
2 tablespoons maple syrup
2 teaspoons grated orange
  zest
½ teaspoon nutmeg or
  cinnamon
Salt and pepper

THIS GRATIN RECIPE came to me while I was on the island of Kauai. I had access to unbelievably sweet oranges at the home I rented, and paired with the yams and apples, it was a marriage made in heaven. I served this dish with a huge green salad that combined both fruits and vegetables, and to top it all off, the Raw Hawaiian Pudding pie (page 178). What a treat!

1. Preheat the oven to 400°F.

2. Drizzle olive oil into a rectangular 9 x 11-inch baking dish. Add sweet potatoes, apples, orange juice, maple syrup, oil, orange zest, and nutmeg. Season with salt and pepper.

3. Stirring every 15 to 20 minutes, allow the gratin to bake approximately 1 hour 15 minutes, or until the sweet potatoes and apples are soft all the way through. You can cover with aluminum foil if the sweet potatoes begin to brown too quickly.

Suzi's Vegetable Slaw

I AM A COLESLAW LOVER. I have changed the recipe many times over the years, but what remains the same are the memories of eating it in the home where I grew up. There's no place like home, as Dorothy would say! Enjoy.

1. In a large bowl, toss the vegetables and apple to combine. In a smaller bowl, whisk together the dressing ingredients and pour over the slaw. Toss again and serve.

SERVES 4

Slaw

1 cup finely chopped cabbage

2 cups finely chopped Napa cabbage

1 cup grated carrot

2 tablespoons grated red onion (optional)

¾ cup grated Brussels sprouts, remove outer leaves and clean

1 grated apple, approximately 1 cup

Dressing

⅓ cup canned coconut milk

1 tablespoon olive oil

1 tablespoon rice vinegar

1 tablespoon maple syrup

1 to 2 tablespoons lime juice (optional)

Pinch each of cinnamon, cumin, and chili powder

Salt and pepper to taste

Twice–Baked Pesto Potatoes

SERVES 4

1 tablespoon olive oil

1 onion, chopped

2 cups sliced mushrooms

½ cup Pesto Sauce (see
   page 200)

2 large baking potatoes,
   prebaked until fork tender

Salt and pepper to taste

½ to 1 cup grated vegan
   cheddar cheese (optional)

THERE ARE TWO WAYS you can prepare this recipe. One is to prebake the potatoes, up to a day ahead, if needed. The other is to bake them, let them cool, and then while they are cooling, prepare the filling. Either way will work, but if time is an issue, consider baking the potatoes the night before you need them.

1. Preheat the oven to 400°F.

2. In a large skillet, heat the olive oil to medium-high. Sauté the onions until soft, about 4 minutes, then add the mushrooms and continue to cook, stirring occasionally, until the mushrooms begin to release their juices, about 3 to 4 minutes. Add in the pesto sauce, stirring well to incorporate.

3. Cut the potatoes in half and scoop out the center, being careful not to cut too deep into the skin of the potato. Add the potato to the pesto and vegetable mixture and stir well to coat.

4. Spoon the potato-pesto mixture back into the potato skins, and transfer to a baking dish. Sprinkle with cheese (optional) and bake for 20 to 30 minutes, or until browned. Serve hot.

Cheesy Spoonbread

A CREAMY, DREAMY alternative to a classic spoonbread, this recipe uses coconut buttermilk to achieve the perfect taste and texture. Whether served on the side or as the main attraction, this is comfort food through and through!

1. Preheat the oven to 375°F. Grease an 8 x 8-inch square baking dish with canola oil.

2. In a large bowl stir together the cornmeal, sea salt, and maple syrup. Bring the water to a boil and pour over the cornmeal mixture. Set aside for 5 to 10 minutes.

3. To make the "buttermilk," combine the coconut milk and lemon juice. Once the coconut mixture has curdled, whisk it together with the Vegenaise in a small bowl until it is smooth. Stir in the cornmeal mixture, baking soda, and baking powder, and then add the corn and cheese.

4. Pour the batter into the prepared baking dish, and bake 30 to 40 minutes. It should be golden brown and firm to the touch. Allow to cool on a wire rack.

SERVES 4 TO 6

1 cup cornmeal

1 teaspoon sea salt

1 tablespoon maple syrup

1⅓ cups boiling water

1 cup coconut milk, regular not light

1 tablespoon lemon juice

¼ cup Follow Your Heart Vegenaise

¾ teaspoon baking soda

2½ teaspoons baking powder

1 cup corn, fresh or frozen

½ cup grated vegan cheddar cheese

Cornbread with Green Chiles

**MAKES ABOUT
12 SQUARES**

1 cup cornmeal

¼ cup coarse cornmeal

½ cup garbanzo bean flour
(chickpea flour)

¼ cup tapioca flour

¼ cup sorghum flour

1½ teaspoons baking
powder

½ teaspoon guar gum

½ teaspoon sea salt

¼ teaspoon cumin

1½ teaspoons Ener-G egg
replacer

2 tablespoons warm water

¾ cup coconut milk (not
canned), or other milk if
preferred, such as hemp
or soy

¼ cup chopped green chile
peppers

2 tablespoons grapeseed oil

I WANTED TO MAKE a cornbread that would look and taste just as good as the one my mom used to make. It took me several attempts to come up with one I thought you would enjoy. I took it around town and had several people try it. They all agreed it was just right. I added cumin to the recipe, but you could also add in chili powder if you like.

1. Preheat the oven to 350°F. Grease an 8 x 8-inch square baking dish with canola oil.

2. Combine the dry ingredients in a small bowl until well blended. In another small bowl, whisk together the egg replacer and water until light and bubbly (frothy) and then add in the coconut milk, green chiles, and grapeseed oil and mix together to fully incorporate.

3. Add the liquid ingredients to the dry ingredients and stir to blend the mixture well.

4. Pour into prepared baking dish. Bake for 20 to 25 minutes or until a toothpick comes out clean. Cool on a wire rack. Cut into squares.

Millet Bread

I WORKED FOR WEEKS to develop a bread that would be worth sharing with you. I love the creamy texture that millet flour provides in this bread. This bread is great for toast, French Toast (page 38), Bruschetta (page 53), and sandwiches.

1. Place the yeast and ½ cup warm water in a large mixing bowl and drizzle 1 teaspoon of the maple syrup over the top. Let this mixture sit until the yeast is bubbly, about 10 minutes. While the yeast is activating, combine all of the dry ingredients in a large bowl. Stir them together really well.

2. In a medium-size bowl, combine the canola oil, pear juice, the rest of the water, and the maple syrup and mix together well.

3. Add the liquid ingredients to the yeast mixture and stir to fully incorporate.

4. Beat on medium speed, adding in the flour mixture until the dough begins to stick together. What you will find with this recipe is that you won't need to use all of the flour. Do not dump all of the flour into the wet ingredients, as you will end up with a dough that is too stiff. Add the flour slowly until your dough holds together but is not wet. I found it is better to have a bit of flour left over to work with when kneading the dough than to end up with an

(continues)

MAKES 1 LOAF

1 package quick-rise yeast

1 cup warm water, divided

¼ cup organic maple syrup, divided

2 cups millet flour

2 cups potato starch

1 cup white rice flour

3 teaspoons guar gum

2 teaspoons baking powder

½ teaspoon sea salt

2 tablespoons canola oil

¾ cup pear juice (or apple juice) room temperature

Millet Bread (continued)

overly dry bread. Next, spread some of the leftover flour mixture onto a surface and knead the dough for 3 minutes or so, until the dough is smooth and not falling apart. Add in more of the flour mixture if you need it.

5. Place the dough in a large bowl and cover. Preheat your oven to 200°F, then when it reaches that temperature, turn it off and open the oven door. Place the bowl on the middle rack of the oven and leave the door slightly ajar. Let the dough rise for about 1 hour.

6. Prep your standard bread pan by lightly spraying with canola or olive oil. When your dough has risen, take it out of the oven and knead it again for a few minutes, then roll it up into a loaf and place in the bread pan. Return it to the oven, or place it in a warm place and let it rise again, this time for about 20 to 25 minutes.

7. Bake in a 350°F oven for about 40 minutes, or until it sounds hollow when tapped lightly on the top. The top of this bread does not naturally brown, so you can either brush the top with olive oil before baking, or put the finished bread under the broiler for a minute to lightly brown. Turn the bread out onto a wire rack and cool completely before slicing.

Sweet Potato Biscuits

I HAVE MADE THESE for gluten-free taste testers as well for my non-gluten-free friends. When the latter group asked for the recipe, I knew I had struck payday! I hope you will enjoy these as much as my taste testers did. These are great served with soup; grilled Portobello Mushroom Steaks (page 140); or for breakfast, served with fruit. You can also serve them with Maple-Pumpkin Butter (page 204) or jam.

1. Preheat the oven to 425°F. Line a cookie sheet with parchment paper.

2. Peel the cooked sweet potato and mash it with a fork on a plate.

3. In a large mixing bowl, combine the following: the flours, baking powder, guar gum, cinnamon, and sea salt.

4. In a separate bowl, whisk together the sweet potato, milk (up to one cup, depending on the texture of the sweet potato), and maple syrup.

5. Cut the palm shortening into the dry ingredients and work it until it is well blended with the dry ingredients. Add the yam and milk mixture and stir together until well blended.

6. Place a large piece of waxed paper on a work surface and pat the dough out onto the waxed

(continues)

MAKES 8 TO 12, DEPENDING ON SIZE

1 cup cooked sweet potato (roasted, boiled, or microwaved)

1½ cups Bob's Red Mill All Purpose Gluten-Free Flour

¼ cup sorghum flour

¼ cup coconut flour

1 tablespoon baking powder

1 teaspoon guar gum (powder or flakes)

1 teaspoon cinnamon

½ teaspoon sea salt

½ to 1 cup So Delicious coconut milk (or soy or hemp milk)

¼ cup organic maple syrup

½ cup organic palm shortening

Sweet Potato Biscuits (continued)

paper, into a ½-inch-thick circle. Using either a biscuit cutter or a glass jar, dip the cutter into flour and then cut biscuits. Evenly place the biscuits on the prepared cookie sheet and bake for 18 to 24 minutes. Cool on a wire rack.

Soups and Salads

Broccoli-Cheese Soup

RICH SOUPS are very comforting, so I came up with a broccoli and cheese soup that I hope will knocks your socks off! I really like the addition of herbes de Provence in this soup, but if you don't have this herb, no worries, just replace it with a bit of rosemary. This recipe takes about one hour to prepare.

1. Heat 1 tablespoon of olive oil in a Dutch oven or stockpot to medium-high and sauté the onion for about 4 minutes, or until soft and translucent. Add in the broccoli and continue to sauté for several minutes, until the broccoli is crisply tender. Add in the garlic and cook 1 minute. Add the red wine and vegetable broth and brewer's yeast and reduce the heat to medium-low and simmer for about 10 minutes.

2. While the soup is simmering, you will make a roux to add to the soup. To do this, heat a small skillet over medium-high heat and add the tablespoon of vegan margarine or virgin coconut oil and when hot, whisk in the arrowroot powder. The mixture will clump together, so you want to begin to add in the coconut milk, whisking quickly, to blend. Keep adding milk while stirring constantly, until the mixture thickens. Add the cheese and stir. It will take about 10 minutes for the cheese mixture to completely melt, so be patient.

(continues)

SERVES 4

- 1 tablespoon extra virgin olive oil
- 2 cups chopped sweet onions
- 5 cups chopped broccoli
- 2 to 3 cloves garlic, minced
- ½ cup red wine (preferably a Cabernet or other fruity wine)
- 3 to 4 cups organic vegetable broth (depending on how thick you like your soup)
- ¼ cup brewer's yeast
- 1 tablespoon vegan olive oil margarine or coconut oil
- 2 teaspoons arrowroot powder
- 1 cup boxed coconut milk (or coconut milk creamer, plain)
- 8 ounces dairy-free cheese (I use Daiya dairy-free, soy-free, grated cheddar shreds)
- 1 teaspoon Dijon mustard
- ½ to 1 teaspoon herbes de Provence
- Big pinch of lemon pepper
- Pinch of red pepper flakes
- ½ teaspoon salt (or to taste)
- Pinch of fresh cracked black pepper

Broccoli-Cheese Soup (continued)

3. Add the cheese mixture to the soup and stir to incorporate well. Season with the mustard, herbes de Provence, lemon pepper, red pepper flakes, salt, and fresh cracked pepper .

4. Let the soup simmer on low for about 10 to 15 minutes, or until the flavors are well blended. I do not purée this soup, but you can if you wish.

Butternut Squash Soup

THIS SOUP IS REALLY nourishing. The coconut milk and spices really warm you up. I pre-bake the butternut squash so the cooking time is reduced. To do this, simply cut the ends off the squash, carefully cut the squash in half lengthwise, and scoop out the seeds in the middle. Preheat the oven to 400°F and place the squash on a greased cookie sheet with an edge (to avoid any juice spilling into your oven). Bake for 40 to 45 minutes, or until a knife inserted into the middle goes through easily.

1. In a Dutch oven or stockpot, heat 1 tablespoon of olive oil over medium-high heat. Add in the onion and sauté until soft, about 4 minutes. Add in the chopped apple and continue to cook for 3 to 4 minutes. Add the bell peppers and cook another 3 minutes, stirring occasionally.

2. Continue to cook until the apple softens, then add in the garlic, spices, cilantro, orange juice, coconut milk, vegetable broth, maple syrup, and prebaked butternut squash.

3. Heat to a boil, then reduce the heat and simmer until the flavors have blended, about 20 minutes. Season with salt and pepper as desired.

SERVES 4 TO 6

1 tablespoon olive oil

1 cup chopped onion (red or yellow)

1 large organic apple (preferably Gala), cored and diced

1 cup chopped red, yellow, or green bell pepper (I use a combo of red and yellow)

1 tablespoon finely chopped garlic

¼ teaspoon cardamom

1 teaspoon cumin

½ teaspoon cinnamon

Pinch of cayenne pepper

½ cup chopped fresh cilantro

¼ cup fresh-squeezed orange juice

½ cup canned coconut milk

1 quart plus 1 cup vegetable broth (organic preferred)

2 tablespoons organic maple syrup

5 cups peeled and chopped butternut squash, prebaked and cut into cubes

Coarse kosher salt, if desired

Fresh cracked pepper to taste

Carrot and Ginger Soup

SERVES 4

1 tablespoon olive oil

1 cup chopped onion

3 cups chopped carrots

1 tablespoon peeled and
    grated ginger

4 cups vegetable broth

1 tablespoon maple syrup or
    agave nectar

1 tablespoon lemon juice

1 teaspoon cumin

¼ teaspoon cinnamon

½ teaspoon ground
    coriander

¼ teaspoon freshly grated
    nutmeg (optional)

Sea salt

Freshly ground black pepper

½ cup vegan sour cream
    (optional)

THIS SOUP HAS WONDERFUL antioxidant properties. It is great to warm the heart and rev up the immune system! If you want to reduce the fat, sauté the onion and carrot in vegetable broth and skip the olive oil altogether. You can also make this soup soy-free by doing the following: Place ⅓ cup raw cashews in a food processor with ¼ cup water. Pulse until ground fine. Add to the soup in place of the soy sour cream.

1. In a Dutch oven or stockpot, heat olive oil over medium-high heat. Add the onion and sauté 3 to 4 minutes or until translucent. Add carrots and ginger and continue sautéing another minute or two, before adding the vegetable broth, maple syrup, and lemon juice. Bring to a boil.

2. Reduce heat to medium and cook until the carrots are tender. Add the cumin, cinnamon, coriander, and nutmeg and season to taste with sea salt and pepper.

3. Using a blender or food processor, purée the soup until it has a smooth and even consistency. Return to stovetop and reheat.

4. Garnish with a dollop of vegan sour cream and a pinch of nutmeg and season with salt and pepper as desired.

Hearty Vegetable Stew

AS THE NAME SAYS, it's hearty—and it's delicious. You can make a huge pot of this and then munch on it for several days. You can serve this stew over rice or by itself.

1. Roast the Brussels sprouts.

2. While the Brussels sprouts are roasting, heat a large stockpot or Dutch oven to medium-high heat and add in the olive oil. When hot, add the onions and carrots and sauté until the onions soften, about 4 minutes.

3. Add in the squash and cook another 4 to 5 minutes, then add the spinach, celery, and garbanzo beans and cook until the spinach is wilted. Add the mushrooms, garlic, steamed green beans, and the red or yellow bell peppers.

4. Add the roasted Brussels sprouts and continue to cook another 2 to 3 minutes. Add the tomato paste, vegetable broth, seasonings, and wine and reduce heat to medium-low. Simmer the stew until the flavors are blended and all of the vegetables are tender, but not overcooked. Season with salt and pepper.

SERVES 6

2 cups Roasted Brussels Sprouts (see page 92)
1 tablespoon olive oil
1 onion, finely chopped (about 1 cup)
1 cup chopped carrot
1 cup chopped butternut squash, peeled and cut into 1-inch pieces
2 cups chopped spinach, stems removed
½ cup chopped celery
2 cups canned garbanzo beans, rinsed and drained
2 cups chopped mushrooms
4 to 6 cloves garlic, peeled and minced
3 cups chopped green beans, cut into ½-inch pieces and steamed
1 cup chopped roasted red and/or yellow bell pepper
1 (4-ounce) can tomato paste
1 cup vegetable broth
¼ cup chopped fresh tarragon
1 teaspoon red chili paste
½ cup white wine (crisp, dry, white wine, with flavors of apple and pear)
Salt and pepper to taste

Homemade Vegetable Stock

**MAKES AT LEAST
2 QUARTS**

10 to 12 cups of water

2 large onions, peeled and
quartered

3 to 4 stalks of celery, leaves
included, roughly
chopped

1 medium-size yam, peeled
and quartered

2 large carrots, cut into large
chunks

1 cup fresh spinach, stems
removed

2 large tomatoes, quartered

½ pound mushrooms,
cleaned

4 or 5 cloves garlic, peeled

1 or 2 bay leaves

½ cup parsley

1 teaspoon dried oregano

1 teaspoon kosher sea salt

½ teaspoon fresh cracked
pepper

THIS BROTH IS GREAT as a base for any of the soups provided in this cookbook, or when broth is requested in other recipes. It makes a fair amount, so you can use some now and put the rest in the refrigerator for another day. You can also freeze this broth for later use. This is a good veggie base, but you can get creative with the herbs and spices as well as the vegetables. In the winter, for instance, I would put in a lot of root vegetables and leave out the tomatoes. I would add in fresh peas and green beans in the summer, and in the fall I would add more tomatoes. Let this recipe be a starting place for you.

1. Place the water in a large stockpot and after you chop all of the veggies, toss them and the mushrooms into the pot and bring to a boil.

2. Add the garlic and herbs. Reduce the heat so that the stock just simmers. Cook for 45 to 60 minutes.

3. Remove the bay leaves. Strain the veggies out of the stock or purée the veggies and mushrooms in a food processor and return to the broth. Season with salt and pepper to taste.

Fresh Corn and Tomato Soup

THIS SOUP IS SIMPLE to make, and it is the epitome of a summer soup, as the fresh corn and tomato combination is just plain delightful! If you don't care for coriander—and some people don't—use fresh basil in this recipe. It will be delicious and you can expand on that, too, and add in some fresh tarragon. If you want to make this a creamy soup, add in some vegan sour cream or canned coconut milk.

1. In a large skillet, heat the oil to medium-high heat and add the onion. Sauté until soft, about 4 minutes. Add in the celery and continue to cook, 1 to 2 minutes. Add the garlic, corn, and tomatoes and cook another 3 to 4 minutes.

2. Add the spices and the water and simmer over medium heat until cooked through and the flavors are blended, about 20 minutes. I like to purée half of the soup in a food processor to make this soup thicker. Season with salt and pepper to taste prior to serving.

SERVES 4

1 tablespoon olive oil
½ cup chopped onions
1 stalk celery, chopped
2 cloves garlic, minced
4 cups fresh corn
4 large tomatoes, cored and chopped
Handful of fresh coriander (or 1 to 2 teaspoons dried coriander)
Dash of cayenne pepper
1 cup water
Salt and fresh ground pepper to taste

Mushroom Soup

SERVES 4

1 ounce dried porcini
    mushrooms
½ ounce dried chanterelle
    mushrooms
1 tablespoon plus
    1 teaspoon olive oil
¼ cup sliced chestnuts
    (packaged or frozen)
1½ cups finely chopped
    onion
1 cup chopped carrots
1 pound fresh cremini
    mushrooms, cleaned,
    de-stemmed, and sliced
    (about 3 cups)
¼ cup white wine (a wine
    with a hint of pear or
    apple, such as a Viognier
    is great in this soup)
3 to 4 cups organic
    vegetable broth
1 tablespoon finely chopped
    garlic
½ cup chopped fresh parsley
2 teaspoons grated orange
    zest
½ to 1 teaspoon kosher salt,
    to taste
¼ to ½ teaspoon freshly
    ground black pepper, to
    taste

THIS SOUP MAY SURPRISE YOU. It is elegant and smooth, and the toasted chestnuts really tip it over the edge. I buy my chestnuts (not to be confused with water chestnuts) at Trader Joe's. If you don't have a store nearby, you may have difficulty finding them. I have made the soup without the chestnuts, and it is still delicious, so don't despair! I use toasted chestnuts, not raw, which are sometimes found in the frozen food section of a store, or in the produce section during the holidays. Buy some when you find them and freeze them, as you will love them in this recipe. This recipe takes about one and a half hours to prepare.

1. In a large bowl, soak the dried mushrooms in 1 cup hot water (or enough to cover the mushrooms) for 30 minutes.

2. Heat a large skillet over medium-high heat and add 1 teaspoon olive oil. Lightly sauté the chestnuts for about 1 to 3 minutes then remove from skillet and set aside.

3. In a large stockpot or Dutch oven, heat 1 tablespoon olive oil to medium-high. Sauté the onions and carrots 4 to 5 minutes, stirring occasionally. Add the cremini mushrooms to the pot. Continue cooking 4 to 5 minutes or until the mushrooms begin to sweat. If vegetables begin to stick, add 1 or 2 tablespoons white wine or vegetable broth and stir.

4. Remove the dried mushrooms from the soaking water, strain the water, and reserve it for later use. Chop the mushrooms and add to the stockpot. Stir, and cook another few moments before adding the garlic. Cook 1 minute and then add the wine, vegetable broth, and soaking water and bring to a boil.

5. Reduce heat to medium-low and allow to simmer 20 to 30 minutes or until mushrooms are cooked and flavors are combined.

6. Allow the soup to cool enough to work with before transferring approximately ½ of the soup to a blender. Purée until smooth, and then return to the pot; add parsley, chestnuts, and orange zest. Season with salt and pepper to taste.

Navy Bean Soup

SERVES 4

2 tablespoons olive oil

1 cup finely chopped red
onion

¾ cup chopped red and
yellow bell pepper

1½ cups chopped carrots

2 cups chopped yams, cut
into 1-inch cubes

¼ cup chopped poblano
pepper

½ to 1 teaspoon minced
garlic

1 pound dried navy beans,
presoaked

2 large tomatoes, chopped,
approximately 1½ cups

2 teaspoons chipotle chili
pepper

1 teaspoon cumin

½ cup chopped cilantro

1 teaspoon salt

½ teaspoon freshly ground
black pepper

4 cups Homemade
Vegetable Stock (see
page 112)

THERE'S NOTHING COZIER than a hot and hearty soup. This recipe makes a ton! Leftovers here we come!

To soak dried beans, place them in large stock-pot and cover with water. Bring to a boil and remove from heat. Leave covered for 1 to 2 hours, then drain.

1. Heat olive oil in a saucepan over medium-high heat. Add onion, bell pepper, carrots, yams, and poblano pepper. Sauté 4 to 5 minutes.

2. Add garlic, beans, tomatoes, chipotle, cumin, cilantro, salt, pepper, and vegetable stock. Bring to a boil, then reduce heat and allow to simmer. Cook approximately 20 to 25 minutes, or until beans are tender and flavors are combined. Season to taste. Soup can be puréed to desired texture or left chunky.

Roasted Asparagus Soup

THIS SOUP DOESN'T TAKE MUCH time to prepare. It is wonderful as a starter, or it can be paired with a hearty salad for a filling dinner. Serve with the Sweet Potato Biscuits found on page 103 or a slice of Millet Bread (page 101). **Note:** if you don't have leeks, go ahead and substitute red onions or scallions.

1. Preheat the oven to 400°F. Wash the asparagus and break away and discard the tough ends. The asparagus can be cut before or after roasting so they are put into the soup in bite-size pieces. Place the asparagus on a baking sheet, and drizzle with olive oil. Season to taste with salt and pepper and mix to coat, arranging the asparagus evenly on the sheet. Roast until fork tender, about 20 to 30 minutes.

2. In a stockpot or Dutch oven, heat the olive oil to medium-high. Sauté the leeks 8 to 10 minutes or until tender, add the garlic and cook another 1 to 2 minutes before adding the asparagus. Sauté an additional 1 minute, then add the vegetable broth, wine, lemon juice, herbs and spices, and simmer for about 10 minutes.

3. Ladle the soup into a blender and purée until smooth. Continue this process until all of the soup is puréed. Return to the stove and heat through. Adjust seasonings if needed.

SERVES 4

3 cups roasted asparagus

2 tablespoons olive oil

2 cups chopped leeks, white part only

2 to 3 cloves minced garlic (approximately 1 tablespoon)

3 to 4 cups vegetable broth

¼ cup white wine (I use Chatter Creek Viognier)

Juice of 1 lemon, or 2 tablespoons

1 tablespoon chopped fresh tarragon

¼ cup chopped fresh Italian parsley

½ teaspoon freshly ground black pepper

½ teaspoon sea salt

Vegetable "Chicken" Soup with Quinoa

SERVES 4

2 tablespoons olive oil

1 cup finely chopped onion

2 cups chopped broccolini or broccoli

1 cup chopped baby red potatoes

1 cup chopped carrots

1 cup chopped cabbage

1 cup peas (fresh or frozen)

¼ cup chopped piquanté or red bell pepper

¼ cup chopped mushrooms (optional)

1 cup chopped zucchini

1 tablespoon chopped garlic

3 cups vegetable broth

2 cups water, or more vegetable broth

1 cup white wine

1 tablespoon vegan chicken broth powder

1 tablespoon dried parsley, or 2 tablespoons fresh chopped

1 teaspoon herbes de Provence

2 bay leaves

¼ cup quinoa

At least ½ teaspoon freshly ground black pepper

VEGAN CHICKEN broth powder may or may not be available in your neighborhood. I found it at my local health food store, but if you can't find it, ask your grocer to order it for you or order it online. If that is not an option for you, then you can use either a vegetable powder or nutritional yeast in place of the chicken broth powder. **Note:** I used a nice crisp Viognier white wine in this recipe, one that is balanced with a hint of pear, peach, apple, and melon.

1. In a large stockpot or Dutch oven, heat the olive oil to medium-high. Sauté the onions until translucent, approximately 4 to 5 minutes, then add broccolini and potatoes. Continue cooking another 5 to 6 minutes, then add the carrots and cabbage. Be sure to stir frequently as you add ingredients to ensure even cooking.

2. Add the peas, peppers, mushrooms, and zucchini, and cook another 4 to 5 minutes. Finally, add the garlic last, cooking a minute longer. Add the vegetable broth, wine, vegan chicken broth powder, herbs, spices, bay leaves, and quinoa.

3. Reduce heat and allow to simmer until quinoa is cooked and vegetables are tender, about 20 minutes. Season generously with black pepper. Remove the bay leaves and serve. The vegan chicken broth powder and vegetable broth should provide adequate sodium, so no need for extra salt, unless desired.

Mock Egg Salad

I USED NORI TOFU in this recipe, but you can use whatever brand you wish. This is great on sandwich bread, served with sliced avocado, sprouts, lettuce, and tomato; rolled up in lettuce wraps; or served in a scoop over a green salad. It takes only 10 minutes to make.

1. Put all of the ingredients in a food processor and pulse for just a few seconds, until blended but not mushy. Season to taste with salt and pepper if desired. This mixture stores well in an airtight container for several days.

SERVES 4

8 ounces extra firm tofu, drained and broken into chunks

1 stalk celery, finely chopped

1 tablespoon finely chopped green onion (or substitute leek)

1 small clove garlic, finely chopped

1 teaspoon canola oil (optional)

½ teaspoon turmeric

¼ cup Vegenaise

Pinch of cayenne pepper

Small pinch of curry powder

¼ to ½ teaspoon sea salt

Freshly ground black pepper

Pasta Salad

SERVES 4 TO 6

4 cups cooked gluten-free
    pasta shells (cooked
    according to package
    directions and drained),
    cooled

¼ cup chopped sun-dried
    tomatoes

1 cup chopped green beans,
    steamed

½ cup chopped red bell
    pepper

12 Kalamata olives, pitted
    and chopped

¾ cup chopped or sliced
    zucchini

2 tablespoons chopped
    green onions (white part
    only)

¼ teaspoon minced garlic

½ cup canned garbanzo
    beans, rinsed and drained

¼ cup Balsamic Vinaigrette
    Dressing (see page 198)

2 tablespoons chopped fresh
    basil

½ teaspoon Redmond
    Organic Seasoning Salt

½ cup chopped parsley

Fresh cracked pepper to
    taste

1 teaspoon dried oregano

1 tablespoon chopped fresh
    tarragon (optional)

THIS IS ONE OF those salads that you can literally make from anything in the refrigerator! I like to use Italian seasoning, but you can experiment with this and use whatever you feel is appropriate. For example, you could make this a southwest pasta salad, using cilantro, black beans, onion, pepper, ancho chilis, cumin, and chili powder, or whatever you like. The possibilities depend on what veggies you have on hand and what spices spark your fancy.

1. Place the cooled pasta in a large bowl and add the following: sun-dried tomatoes, green beans, red bell pepper, olives, zucchini, green onions, garlic, and garbanzo beans.

2. In a large jar or bowl, whisk together really well the following: balsamic dressing, fresh basil, seasoning salt, parsley, fresh cracked pepper, oregano, and tarragon.

3. When fully blended, toss the pasta ingredients with dressing. If the salad is too dry, add more dressing to taste. Season to taste.

Roasted Beet and Arugula Salad

I NEVER LIKED BEETS as a kid, but boy do I love them now! If you preroast your beet, this is a very quick recipe to make. I try to roast a few beets at a time, so I have one handy in the refrigerator.

I find the combination of beets, arugula, and grapefruit to be a refreshing assortment, but you can also add in watercress, mixed greens, and other fruits, such as peaches or apples.

1. Set a small bowl on the counter, and holding the grapefruit over the bowl, peel it and then pull it apart into segments (you are using the bowl to catch any juice that escapes in this process). Cut the grapefruit segments in half (on a cutting board, not over the bowl) and place in a large bowl. If no juice escaped from the grapefruit when pulling apart, squeeze one of the segments into the small bowl, so you have some juice.

2. Then, add the oil, sherry vinegar, maple syrup, and mustard to the grapefruit juice. Whisk this mixture really well until it is thick and creamy. If you need to add more juice, squeeze another segment of grapefruit into the bowl.

3. Chop the roasted beet and add it to the large bowl with the grapefruit sections. Add in the arugula leaves and pour the oil and vinegar mixture over the top and toss to coat evenly. Season with salt and freshly cracked pepper to taste.

SERVES 4

½ pink grapefruit, peeled and cut into bite-size pieces
2 to 3 tablespoons olive oil
1 tablespoon sherry vinegar
2 teaspoons organic maple syrup
1 teaspoon Dijon mustard
1 roasted beet (see page 93 for roasting instructions)
2 bunches of arugula leaves, torn into edible bites (3 cups)
½ cup Candied Nuts (see page 62)
¼ teaspoon kosher sea salt
Fresh cracked pepper to taste

Note: To add protein to this dish, add pine nuts or pecans.

Sheila's Favorite Avocado and Corn Salad

SERVES 4

1 large avocado, peeled,
    pitted, and cut into small
    cubes
2 cups chopped tomatoes,
    cleaned, cored, and de-
    stemmed
⅓ cup torn fresh basil leaves
2 cups white or yellow corn
    (fresh is best, but
    otherwise, frozen)
¼ teaspoon sea salt or
    kosher salt
¼ cup chopped raw cashews
Lots of fresh cracked pepper
¼ cup extra virgin olive oil
2 tablespoons sherry vinegar
1 teaspoon Dijon mustard

I SERVED THIS RECIPE to my friend who came over to taste test some of my recipes. She said this was her favorite, and that I needed to name it something really special because she thought it was fabulous. Well, I am. I am naming it after my fabulous friend Sheila! You might want to double this recipe, as it won't last long; it's so good it's addictive!

Note: This recipe can also be served as an appetizer. I love to serve this with brown rice chips.

1. Mix all the ingredients together except for the olive oil, sherry vinegar, and mustard. In a separate small bowl, whisk together the oil, sherry vinegar, and mustard until the mixture thickens slightly. Pour this over the salad mixture and toss. Place the salad in the refrigerator (covered) for up to 1 hour to allow the flavors to mix. Serve chilled.

Spinach Salad

THIS IS SUCH a refreshing salad! I love the crunch of the nuts, the sweetness of the strawberries, and the tanginess of the dressing. This salad is perfect for a summer dinner on the back deck. If you don't have any fresh strawberries in the house, you can easily substitute raspberries, marionberries, or blueberries.

1. Place the dressing ingredients in a small bowl or glass jar and whisk together really well (or place a lid on the jar and shake vigorously) until mixture is completely blended.

2. Tear the spinach leaves and place in a large salad bowl. Add the pear, strawberries, nuts, onion, and avocado. Add the salad dressing and toss to coat. Do not use all of the dressing to begin with, but start with a small amount and then add more if needed. If you have dressing left over, store in the refrigerator in an airtight container; it will last several days.

SERVES 4

Dressing

3 tablespoons olive oil

2 tablespoons balsamic vinegar

1 teaspoon Dijon mustard

1 tablespoon maple syrup

¼ teaspoon coarse kosher salt

Fresh cracked pepper

Salad

1 bunch of fresh spinach, stems removed

1 pear (Bosc or Bartlett), cored and sliced

1 cup chopped fresh strawberries, cut in half, stems removed

1 cup caramelized nuts (pecans or almonds)

½ cup thinly sliced red onion

1 avocado, peeled, pitted, and chopped or sliced

Family Classics

Barbara's Special Marinated Tempeh

TEMPEH IS A FIBER-RICH soy protein. My dear friend Barbara developed this recipe and shared it with me. What I loved about it was how quick it was to make and how easy too. It is satisfying alone or alongside a tossed green salad.

1. Whisk the following together in a 9 x 9-inch square dish: maple syrup, tamari, rice vinegar, and cayenne pepper.

2. After you mix the marinade, slice the tempeh into about 14 pieces and lay it out in the dish to soak in the marinade. Let marinate for 30 minutes, turning over at least once before cooking. Reserve any remaining marinade.

3. Heat a large skillet over medium high-heat and add 1 tablespoon coconut oil. Sauté the onions until they begin to soften, about 3 minutes. Add the green beans and cook until they are crisp-tender, an additional 4 to 5 minutes. Add the garlic and sauté 1 to 2 minutes. Remove the vegetables from the skillet and place in a bowl.

4. Return the skillet to the heat and add 1 tablespoon coconut oil. When the oil is hot, add several slices of tempeh and sauté 3 to 4 minutes on each side. If all of the slices fit in the skillet at once, great, but if not, sauté in batches until all are cooked. Add the green bean mixture to the skillet with the tempeh and pour any remaining marinade over the top. Heat through and serve hot.

SERVES 4

3 tablespoons maple syrup

3 tablespoons gluten-free tamari

2 teaspoons rice vinegar

¼ teaspoon cayenne pepper

1 (8-ounce) package gluten-free organic tempeh, sliced

2 tablespoons organic virgin coconut oil

1 cup finely chopped onion

3 cups chopped green beans, ends removed

1 teaspoon (or more as desired) minced garlic

Black Bean Burgers, Kristine-Style

MAKES 4 BURGERS

1 (15-ounce) can of organic
black beans, washed and
drained (or 2 cups fresh
beans, soaked, drained,
and cooked per package
directions)

2 teaspoons dried parsley (or
¼ cup finely chopped
fresh cilantro)

3 tablespoons finely
chopped onions

1 carrot, finely chopped or
grated

1 teaspoon chia seeds
whisked together well
with 2 tablespoons water
(let sit 5 to 10 minutes,
then whisk again before
adding to food processor)

1 teaspoon sea salt

½ teaspoon cumin

1 teaspoon chili powder (or
chipotle pepper)

1 teaspoon minced garlic

⅓ cup sorghum flour

Up to 2 tablespoons olive oil

I LOVE BLACK BEANS, so I developed this recipe and sent it off to one of my recipe testers. Kristine and her husband played around with my original recipe and made it even better, so I decided to name it after her. You can serve them with fresh guacamole, salsa, and hummus, with or without a bun, or you can create a lettuce wrap and add all of the trimmings of a burger. Try the Avocado Mayo found on page 197. You can add a squeeze of lime juice and serve with a Tex-Mex rice. Get creative with this—the possibilities are vast! If you prefer not to fry these burgers, you can also throw them on the grill or bake them.

1. Wash and drain the beans and then place them in a food processor and pulse to mash only partway at this point, so they are half mashed.

2. Next, add in the rest of the ingredients, except for the flour and olive oil. Pulse until mixture is well blended, and then remove from processor and place in a large bowl, so you can work with the ingredients better.

3. Add in the flour and form the mixture into burger-size patties. I recommend washing your hands and then picking up a handful of the mixture and forming it into a ball. Then, press it out on a piece of waxed paper until you have a patty. You should end up with 4 patties.

4. Heat a skillet to medium-high and add in ½ tablespoon of olive oil. When hot, place a patty in the skillet and cook it for about 4 minutes on each side. You want the patty to be crisp on the outside but not too mushy on the inside, so if you need to cook the patty a bit longer, reduce the heat and continue to cook another minute or two. Continue this process until you have cooked all 4 patties. You can use a larger skillet if you wish and cook them all at once.

Eggplant Parmesan

2 large eggplants, peeled
 and sliced into ¼-inch
 thick slices

Olive oil to brush on
 eggplant

1 (15-ounce) can organic
 tomato sauce (or 2 cups of
 fresh sauce)

¼ cup red wine (Cabernet
 works great in this recipe)

3 tablespoons chopped fresh
 basil

1 teaspoon dried oregano

¼ teaspoon cinnamon

1 teaspoon kosher salt

½ teaspoon minced garlic
 (or as much as you like,
 up to 1 tablespoon)

¼ to ½ teaspoon fresh
 cracked pepper

1 (10-ounce) package either
 soy or rice mozzarella
 cheese

I ESPECIALLY LOVE eggplant parmesan, so I was determined to make a version that not only I would love, but so would you. If you don't care for soy cheese, use rice cheese. There are good mozzarella imitations available at most health food stores. Be sure you read the ingredients, as some cheese alternatives actually include casein as an ingredient, and that comes from cows.

This recipe takes about one and a half hours start to finish. Well worth the wait.

Note: Eggplants have a lot of water in them, so if you wish to reduce the liquid that may result while cooking, slice the eggplants into ¼-inch slices, then lightly salt each slice and drain on paper towels. You will be amazed at how much moisture is absorbed by the paper towels. Let the slices sit on the towels for about 15 minutes, then flip over and salt the other side. Wash the eggplants to remove excess salt before using in the recipe. I skip this step if I am grilling the eggplants, as I find the grilling process removes the excess moisture from the eggplants.

1. Depending on what time of year it is, you have 2 options for beginning this recipe. First, if it is summer, break out the barbeque, as you can grill the eggplant. To do that, lightly coat your eggplant slices with olive oil. Place on the hot grill and cook for a few minutes on each side until nicely browned. Remove from heat and take inside.

Sheila's Favorite Avocado and
Corn Salad (page 122)

Suzi's Vegetable Slaw
(page 97)

**Black-Bean Burgers
Kristine-Style (page 128)**

Meatless Meatballs (page 139),
Garlic Mashed Potatoes (page 88),
and Mushroom Gravy with Red Wine (page 91)

Pizza (page 73)

My Favorite Lasagna
(page 137)

Peanut Butter–Chocolate Chip Fudge
(page 64)

Chocolate Cupcakes
(page 77)

2. Now, if it's not summer or you don't have a grill, try option **2.** If you own a George Foreman Grill, turn that on and let it heat up. Prep your eggplant as directed previously only this time, you don't have to go outside. Place a few slices at a time on the grill and cook until each side is nicely browned.

3. If you don't have either option, then I would recommend broiling the eggplant.

4. While you are cooking/grilling your eggplant, put all of the remaining ingredients, except the cheese, together in a medium-size bowl to allow the flavors to blend. Grate the mock cheese and set aside.

5. Once you have prepped your eggplant the fun begins. Preheat the oven to 350°F and then lightly oil a 9 x 9-inch square baking dish. Pour a small amount of the sauce into the baking dish. Now, layer some of the eggplant over the sauce and then spread some of the grated cheese over the top of that layer. Add some more sauce, then eggplant, then cheese and keep going until you run out of everything. Be sure to save enough cheese to sprinkle over the top of the dish. Crack some fresh pepper over the top and then pop it into the oven and cook for about 35 to 45 minutes, or until the mixture is bubbly.

Fresh Pea and Asparagus Risotto

SERVES 4

1 to 2 tablespoons olive oil

1 cup finely chopped onion

1 cup chopped asparagus, ends cut off and chopped into 1-inch pieces

½ cup chopped red or yellow bell pepper

½ cup chopped fresh arugula leaves

1 cup fresh peas

¾ cup Arborio rice

4 to 5 cups vegetable stock

½ cup white wine (Use a wine that has clean flavors, including peach, pear, melon, and apple. A Viognier would work nicely)

2 teaspoons lemon juice

1 tablespoon lemongrass (optional)

1 tablespoon finely chopped garlic (2 or 3 large cloves)

Pinch of lemon pepper

1 tablespoon dried tarragon (optional)

¼ teaspoon grated zest of lemon

Salt and pepper to taste

I HAVE MADE many versions of this popular rice dish over the years and fresh peas and asparagus are a perfect springtime combination. I make this entirely without any mock cheese, as I find that "cheese" made from soy or rice has a flavor that would mask the wonderful fresh flavors of these vegetables. If you have other veggies that you want to add to this recipe, by all means, do so. This is a perfect meal to serve with a simple salad and/or fruit. If you wish to add protein to this dish, toss in some toasted pine nuts or walnuts.

1. In a large Dutch oven or stockpot, heat 1 tablespoon of the olive oil and then add the onion and sauté until soft, about 4 minutes. Add in the asparagus and continue to cook for an additional 3 to 4 minutes. If you need more oil, to avoid sticking, add the additional tablespoon of oil. Add in the bell pepper and arugula and sauté for 2 to 3 minutes. Add the peas in last. Remove the vegetables from the pan and set aside in a bowl.

2. Turn the heat back up to medium-high and when the Dutch oven is hot, add the rice and toast it for a minute or so, stirring the rice around.

3. Heat the vegetable broth in a stockpot until it is boiling. Keep the broth very hot, at a constant simmer while you are preparing the risotto.

4. Add a ladle full of hot vegetable broth to the rice and stir it around constantly, until the rice has absorbed the broth. You should keep the heat on the rice pan at about medium, so that it is cooking the liquid, but not too hot so that the broth evaporates and isn't absorbed by the rice. This entire process takes about 40 minutes, as you must continue to add each ladle full of broth, stirring constantly, until the rice absorbs the broth, then add another ladle full.

5. When you run out of broth to add to the rice, add in the wine and lemon juice and stir until they are absorbed. Then reduce the heat and add in the vegetables, herbs, lemon zest, spices, and salt and pepper to taste.

Layered Polenta

SERVES 8

2½ cups crushed tomatoes
or tomato sauce

2 cloves garlic, chopped

1 teaspoon dried oregano

½ teaspoon fresh cracked
pepper

¼ cup fresh packed basil
leaves

¼ cup chopped fresh parsley

¼ cup red wine, plus
1 tablespoon

1 tablespoon organic extra
virgin olive oil

1 cup chopped onions

⅓ cup finely chopped sun-
dried tomatoes

½ cup chopped roasted red
bell pepper

1 cup sliced mushrooms

1 small zucchini, chopped
(about 1½ cups)

2 tablespoons pine nuts

Salt to taste

1 (18-ounce) package of
precooked basil garlic
polenta, sliced into
6 slices lengthwise

½ cup vegan cheddar cheese
(rice or soy)

HERE I WANTED TO CREATE something that would be easy and filling. I know that some of you may be appalled that I am using store-bought polenta, but the brand I purchased is organic, and it's vegan and dairy-free. So, I skipped the step of making the polenta myself, but if you prefer to make your own and you have the time, please do! For the red wine, a well-balanced, complex wine with hints of black fruit, red pepper, and plums works well in this recipe. I used a Mendoza Celebration. This dish is super easy to make and really is wonderful served alongside a fresh green salad. *Mangia!*

1. In a large bowl, combine the crushed tomatoes or tomato sauce, garlic, oregano, pepper, basil, parsley, and red wine (minus 1 tablespoon) and set aside to allow flavors to blend.

2. In a large skillet or sauté pan, heat the oil and add the onions. When the onions are soft, about 4 minutes, add in the sun-dried tomatoes and stir. Continue to cook for about 2 minutes, then add the bell pepper, mushrooms, zucchini, pine nuts and cook another 3 to 4 minutes, adding in the tablespoon of wine if needed, to avoid sticking, stirring occasionally. When the veggies are cooked, but not mushy, turn off the stove. Season to taste with salt and additional pepper, if desired.

3. Preheat the oven to 350°F and slice the polenta.

4. Pour a ladle full of the sauce on the bottom of an 8½ x 5-inch glass baking dish. Add 3 slices of the polenta, and lay them lengthwise in the dish. Layer some of the vegetable mixture on top, then sprinkle half of the cheese over the mixture. Add another layer of sauce, then another layer of polenta, then the vegetables, then sauce and finally, the cheese. Bake in the oven, uncovered for 30 to 40 minutes, or until the casserole is bubbly. Let stand at room temperature for 5 minutes before serving.

Mock Tuna Fish Sandwich Fixin's

**MAKES ABOUT 2 CUPS;
ABOUT 4 SERVINGS ON
SANDWICHES OR IN
LETTUCE WRAPS**

1 (15-ounce) can organic
   garbanzo beans
1 dill pickle, chopped fine
¼ cup finely chopped red
   bell pepper or sweet
   piquanté pepper
¼ cup finely chopped celery
2 tablespoons minced carrot
2 tablespoons vegan mayo
1 teaspoon lemon juice
   (fresh, if possible)
1 teaspoon Dijon mustard
   (less if you prefer)
1 teaspoon pickle juice
Salt and fresh cracked
   pepper to taste

I LIKE TO SERVE this as an open-faced sandwich on gluten-free bread, with tomatoes and avocado on top. You can also use it in a lettuce wrap or just as it is. I would recommend you toast the Millet Bread found on page 101 and top it with this mixture and tomatoes. A wonderful way to get your afternoon protein. I use Follow Your Heart Vegenaise mayo.

1. Rinse the beans, then place in a food processor and pulse for about 20 to 30 seconds, until mashed. Place in a bowl and add the rest of the ingredients. Stir to fully incorporate the ingredients and then season with salt and pepper.

My Favorite Lasagna

I LOVE ARTICHOKE HEARTS, sun-dried tomatoes, mushrooms, and spinach, so this recipe has become one of my favorites! You can use whatever veggies you have in the house in this dish.

1. Lightly spray a 9 x 12-inch baking dish with olive oil.

2. Reconstitute the porcini mushrooms by putting them in a bowl and covering with 1 cup hot water. Let soak for 30 minutes. Reserve the water for use in the recipe.

3. In a large skillet or Dutch oven, heat the olive oil over medium high heat. When the oil is hot, add the onions and sauté for 4 minutes. Add in ¼ cup of the saved mushroom broth, the carrots, and artichoke hearts and sauté another 4 to 5 minutes. Add in the bell peppers, piquanté peppers, and sun-dried tomatoes and sauté 1 to 2 minutes. Add the spinach and garlic and sauté another 2 to 3 minutes. Add in the tomato sauce and following herbs: basil, 1 teaspoon of the tarragon, parsley, salt and ¼ teaspoon pepper) and then remove from heat.

4. In a clean skillet, add ¼ cup of the mushroom broth and then add both the cremini and porcini mushrooms and sauté for several minutes, until the mushrooms are soft and they have released their juices.

5. While the mushrooms are cooking, combine the following in a small bowl: ¼ cup white wine, ¼ cup

SERVES 6 TO 8

- ½ cup dried porcini mushrooms
- 1 tablespoon olive oil
- 2 cups finely chopped onions
- 1 cup reserved water from mushrooms
- 2 large carrots, either chopped or grated (about 1 cup)
- 1 (14-ounce) can of artichoke hearts, chopped (about 1¼ cups)
- ½ cup sliced roasted red and/or yellow bell peppers
- ½ cup chopped pickled piquanté peppers (I use Peri-Peri Peppadrops from Trader Joe's)
- 1 cup sun-dried tomatoes
- 1 cup hot water
- 4 cups chopped fresh spinach
- 2 to 3 cloves garlic, minced
- 1 (15-ounce) can tomato sauce (nearly 2 cups fresh sauce)

(continues)

My Favorite Lasagna (continued)

½ cup torn or chopped basil leaves

2 teaspoons dried tarragon, divided

1 tablespoon dried parsley

1 scant teaspoon sea salt

½ teaspoon fresh cracked pepper, divided

4 cups cleaned and sliced cremini mushrooms, stems removed

¼ cup white wine (I use Pinot Grigio, but you could also use a Viognier)

1 (8-ounce) package Tofutti cream cheese

½ teaspoon dried oregano

2 tablespoons nutritional yeast

1 teaspoon arrowroot powder

½ package Tinkyada gluten-free lasagna noodles (about 8 noodles)

mushroom broth, and the cream cheese. Whisk this mixture together really well until it is smooth and creamy. Add in 1 teaspoon tarragon, ½ teaspoon oregano, 2 tablespoons of nutritional yeast, and a pinch of fresh cracked pepper. Whisk together well and then add this to the mushrooms.

6. Bring this mixture to a slow boil and then add in the arrowroot powder. Cook for 1 minute and then reduce the heat to low and continue to cook until thickened.

7. Preheat the oven to 350°F. On the stovetop, prepare the noodles according to the package directions and then drain.

8. To put your lasagna together, place a layer of noodles across the bottom of the prepared dish. Cover the noodles with the vegetable mixture, then a layer of the mushroom sauce, then grated cheese. Do this again, until you have used up all of the veggies, mushroom sauce, and cheese. Be sure to end with enough cheese to lightly cover the top.

9. Bake uncovered for about 30 minutes, or until lasagna is bubbly. Remove from heat and let stand 5 minutes before serving.

Meatless Meatballs

MEATBALLS ARE DEFINITELY a comfort food. Here a combination of nuts, mushrooms, and mashed potatoes replace the meat. These are great served with spaghetti.

1. Spray a baking sheet with a small amount of olive oil or line it with parchment paper.

2. In a large skillet, sauté the onions and the walnuts in the oil over medium-high heat, until the onions are soft, about 4 minutes. Add in the mushrooms and continue to cook until the mushrooms are soft and their juices begin to release, about 4 to 5 minutes. Add in the garlic, Bragg Liquid Aminos, water, red wine, dried parsley, oregano, and tamarind sauce.

3. Remove from heat and place this mixture in a food processor. Pulse for about 30 seconds. Add in the cornflakes and chia seed mixture and pulse another 15 seconds or so.

4. Place this mixture in a large bowl and work in the mashed potatoes, using either a wooden spoon or clean hands. When mixture is well incorporated, roll into balls.

5. Heat the oven to 350°F. Place the balls on the prepared baking sheet and bake for 20 minutes. Turn the balls over and bake another 20 minutes.

Note: Most Worcestershire sauces contain anchovies, so if you can't find a vegan version, use tamarind sauce.

MAKES 6 MEATLESS MEATBALLS

1 tablespoon olive oil

¾ to 1 cup chopped raw walnuts

⅔ cup finely chopped onions

2 cups chopped and cleaned mushrooms

½ teaspoon minced garlic (1 clove)

1 tablespoon Bragg Liquid Aminos

1 tablespoon water

1 tablespoon red wine (I use a medium-bodied wine with hints of blackberry or current, such as a Barbera)

¼ cup dried parsley flakes

1 teaspoon dried oregano

1 teaspoon vegan Worcestershire sauce or tamarind sauce

½ cup mashed potatoes

¼ cup finely crushed gluten-free cornflakes (or rice crackers)

1 teaspoon chia seeds whisked together really well with 2 tablespoons warm water

Portobello Mushroom Steak
with Smothered Onions

SERVES 4

4 portobello mushrooms,
   stems removed, cleaned
½ cup extra virgin olive oil
¼ cup red wine
3 cloves garlic, minced
2 teaspoons tamarind sauce
1 teaspoon blackstrap
   molasses
2 teaspoons balsamic
   vinegar
½ teaspoon kosher sea salt
¼ teaspoon fresh cracked
   pepper
1 tablespoon olive oil
1 large onion, peeled and
   sliced thinly (about 2 cups)
1 tablespoon arrowroot
   powder (optional)

THIS RECIPE is one of my very favorites. I love the flavors in the sauce that the mushrooms marinate in. For the red wine, select a wine that is full bodied, with hints of berries and smoke, such as a Cabernet or Syrah. I also love the taste created when the mushrooms are cooked over a hot grill. Serve these steaks with a side of mashed sweet potatoes, roasted asparagus, and a green salad. Nothing says "heaven" more than this!

1. In a casserole dish large enough to hold all four mushrooms, mix together the extra virgin olive oil, red wine, garlic, tamarind sauce, molasses, balsamic vinegar, salt, and pepper. Whisk the mixture together well.

2. Add the mushrooms to the marinade, gill side up. With a spoon, drizzle some of the marinade over the top of the mushrooms and let sit for about 15 minutes. Flip the mushrooms over and marinate on the other side for another 10 to 15 minutes. Do not discard the marinade when you grill the mushrooms, as you can use it as a sauce to finish the dish.

3. Heat a large skillet to medium-high, add a small amount of olive oil and sauté the onion until soft and lightly browned, about 8 to 10 minutes, stirring often. If the onions begin to stick to the skillet, add a bit more oil, or some veggie broth. If the onions do not all fit in your skillet, then sauté them in batches until they are all cooked. You want to end up with nicely browned onions that will be draped over your mushroom steaks.

4. Heat a barbeque grill to high heat and when hot, set the mushrooms on the grill. Cook on each side about 3 to 5 minutes. The mushrooms will release their juices when they are cooked. Be sure they are fully cooked, but not mushy.

5. If you wish, you can heat the reserved marinade in a saucepan to medium-high heat. When the sauce comes to a boil, add in 1 tablespoon arrowroot powder and whisk briskly to incorporate. Reduce heat to low and cook for a minute or 2 until the mixture thickens slightly. You do not need to do this step if you don't want to; the marinade is great drizzled over the top of the mushrooms just as it is.

Pumpkin Pizza Crust

**ONE 9-INCH TO 10-INCH
PIZZA CRUST**

1 teaspoon chia seeds

1 cup warm water, divided

1 teaspoon yeast

1 cup brown rice flour

1 cup sorghum flour

½ cup tapioca starch

1 teaspoon guar gum

¼ teaspoon sea salt

½ cup cooked canned
    pumpkin

2 tablespoons maple syrup

¼ cup canola oil

PUMPKIN PIZZA CRUST? Who would think of such a thing? This recipe is definitely not traditional, but it makes for a delicious pizza!

1. In a small bowl, whisk together the chia seeds and 2 tablespoons of the water until they begin to gel together. Let this mixture sit for about 10 minutes.

2. Mix the dry ingredients together in a large bowl. In a medium-size bowl, combine the rest of the water, the pumpkin, maple syrup, canola oil, and chia seed mixture. Whisk together really well to blend. Slowly add the wet ingredients to the dry ingredients and stir together with a wooden spoon. Cover the mixture and let it sit for about 10 minutes in a warm place.

3. While you wait, prepare your pizza toppings and sauce (see recipe on page 73).

4. Press the dough mixture onto a pizza pan (I use a Brazilian soapstone pizza stone) or large cookie sheet and shape into a circle. Place your sauce and toppings over the crust and bake in a 400°F oven until done, about 30 minutes.

Roasted Beet Risotto

IF YOU LIKE BEETS, you will love this! The recipe for roasting the beets can be found on page 93. The combo of the coarse kosher salt and fresh cracked pepper with the Zinfandel wine is just delicious. This dish is great leftover—if it lasts that long!

1. In a large skillet, heat the olive oil to medium-high and add the onion. Cook until it softens, about 4 minutes. Add in the minced garlic and stir well. Cook for 1 minute, stirring constantly. Remove this mixture from the pan and place in a bowl. Set aside.

2. Return the skillet to the burner and heat it back up to medium-high. Add in the rice and toast it slightly for a minute or so. Simultaneously, heat the vegetable broth and wine in a stockpot over high heat until they begin to boil; then reduce the heat so that the mixture continues to simmer.

3. Add a ladle full of stock and wine to the rice mixture and stir until it is incorporated. You are going to need to stand at the stove for about 40 minutes or so, so get comfy! Once the liquid is absorbed by the rice, add another ladle full of stock and wine. Continue this process until the rice is cooked and you are out of vegetable stock/wine.

4. Add in the onion-garlic mixture, the roasted beets (chopped), spices, toasted walnuts, salt, and pepper and heat the mixture over medium-low heat, allowing the flavors to blend. Season to taste, if desired, and serve hot.

SERVES 4 TO 6

1 tablespoon olive oil
1 cup finely chopped onion
1 teaspoon minced garlic
¾ cup Arborio rice
2 cups vegetable broth (homemade is best, but organic boxed is OK too in a pinch)
2 cups red fruity wine, such as Zinfandel
2 cups chopped roasted beets (see recipe on page 93)
¼ teaspoon fresh grated nutmeg
¼ teaspoon lemon pepper
¼ teaspoon chili powder
½ cup chopped toasted walnuts (or other nuts, such as pine nuts or pecans)
½ teaspoon coarse kosher salt or sea salt
½ teaspoon fresh cracked pepper
Drizzle of truffle oil (totally optional!)

Savory Spinach Pie

1 recipe Nutty Piecrust (see page 183)

1 (12.3-ounce) box silken extra firm tofu, drained

1 tablespoon olive oil

1 cup finely chopped onions

1 cup chopped roasted red and yellow bell pepper (from a jar or roasted ahead of time)

½ pound mushrooms (cremini or other) cleaned, de-stemmed, and sliced (about 3 cups)

2 tablespoons vegetable broth

1 large bunch of fresh spinach (about 5 cups chopped), stems cut off

¼ cup chopped fresh basil (or 1 tablespoon dried)

1 teaspoon dried oregano

½ teaspoon dried tarragon

1 teaspoon Bragg herb seasoning

Large pinch of cinnamon

1 cup grated mock mozzarella cheese (rice cheese)

½ to 1 teaspoon coarse kosher salt

Lots of fresh cracked pepper (about ½ teaspoon)

MY SON RORY inspired me to make this recipe. He wanted me to use the Nutty Piecrust for something other than desserts. When I came up with this recipe, most all of my taste testers loved it! There was one though, my friend Peter, who thought the piecrust was good, but too sweet for a savory dish such as this. So, it's up to you. You might consider removing maple syrup from the crust recipe (this won't affect its texture) when making this delicious alternative to spinach and mushroom quiche. You can make the piecrust a day ahead if you wish.

1. Prebake the Nutty Piecrust and then cool.

2. Place the tofu in a food processor and pulse on high until the tofu is smooth and creamy—no lumps. This will take up to 1 minute to really make this a nice consistency. Set aside.

3. In a large skillet, heat the oil to medium-high and add in the onions. Sauté until soft, about 4 to 5 minutes. Add in the peppers and mushrooms and vegetable broth and continue to cook another 4 or 5 minutes. Add the spinach and sauté until wilted, about 3 to 4 minutes. Lower the heat and add in the herbs, herb seasoning, puréed tofu mixture, cinnamon, grated cheese, and simmer for a minute or two, then season with salt and pepper. Pour mixture into the prebaked piecrust and bake at 350°F for 30 minutes. This dish stores well in the fridge, covered, for several days.

Vegetable Potpie

THERE IS NOTHING that compares to home-made potpies! While these look complicated to make, they really aren't. The effort truly pays off when you see the happiness on the faces of those you are feeding.

1. Make the filling. In a Dutch oven or large stockpot heat 1 tablespoon olive oil to medium-high. Add potatoes and yams and cook until tender, approximately 9 to 10 minutes. Add onion, carrots, broccoli, and green beans and continue cooking until broccoli is crisp-tender. If vegetables begin to stick, add a small amount of vegetable stock to deglaze the pan. Add the spinach and mushrooms and cook another 5 minutes or until the juices from the mushrooms release. Set aside.

2. Make the biscuits. In a large mixing bowl, combine brown rice flour, potato starch, baking powder, sea salt, and sugar. Cut in the palm shortening with a pastry cutter or fork, until it is well blended. Add in the milk and stir with a wooden spoon until it is well incorporated. Using clean hands, form the mixture into a large ball and set aside.

3. Make the sauce. Add the olive oil to a large skillet and heat to medium. When the oil is hot, add in the arrowroot powder and whisk it around. It will "ball up quickly" so you need to add in the red wine and continue to whisk it until it is smooth. Add in the vegetable broth and stir constantly, until the mixture thickens. Turn down the

SERVES 6 TO 8

Filling

1 tablespoon extra virgin olive oil

3 cups chopped new potatoes, cut into 1-inch cubes

1 cup chopped yam

1 large onion (about 1 cup finely chopped)

3 large carrots (about 1 ¼ cups chopped)

3 cups chopped broccoli

1 cup chopped fresh green beans, cut into 1-inch segments

Vegetable broth, as needed to prevent sticking (optional)

2 cups chopped fresh spinach

2 cups cleaned and sliced mushrooms, stems removed

(continues)

Vegetable Potpie *(continued)*

Biscuits

2½ cups brown rice flour

1 ½ cups potato starch

1 tablespoon baking powder

1 teaspoon sea salt

¼ cup organic sugar or
    coconut palm sugar

⅔ cup palm shortening

1 cup coconut milk (or soy or
    hemp milk)

Sauce

1 tablespoon extra virgin
    olive oil

2 tablespoons arrowroot
    powder

½ cup red wine (I use
    Chatter Creek Cabernet,
    but any full-bodied red
    wine will do)

½ cup vegetable broth

⅛ teaspoon dried thyme

¼ teaspoon fennel seed
    (optional)

¼ teaspoon cinnamon

½ teaspoon fresh cracked
    pepper

Salt to taste

heat so the mixture does not become too thick and season with the thyme, fennel seed, cinnamon, and fresh cracked pepper. Add salt, if desired.

4. Simmer the sauce over low heat for a minute or two, then add in the filling ingredients and stir to combine mixture. Turn off the heat and spoon the vegetable mixture into either 6 ramekins for individual potpies, or a 9-inch baking dish for one large pie. (You can use a pie dish or oblong dish for this, whatever you prefer if you don't have any ramekins).

5. Preheat oven to 350°F.

6. Lightly flour a work surface with brown rice flour and press the biscuit dough ball out onto the surface, using your hands. Roll out your biscuit dough and cut to fit the top of your ramekins or baking dish. I prefer to use ramekins and cut my dough using a water glass, so the round fits perfectly over the top of the 3-inch ramekin. I pinch the dough over the top of the dish, so it will not pop off while baking.

7. Bake for about 20 minutes, or until the gravy is bubbling and the biscuits are slightly browned (they don't rise, but they sure taste good with the gravy!)

Ethnic Favorites

Banana and Macadamia Nut Curry

I DEVELOPED THIS RECIPE while visiting Hawaii; I love the little apple bananas they have there. I wish we had them back here in Washington State, but I have never seen them. If you have apple bananas at your disposal, I highly recommend them for this recipe. Otherwise, regular bananas work just fine. I suggest serving this curry over Lundberg Farms Festive Red Rice. It has a wonderful texture that pairs brilliantly with this dish.

1. In a large stockpot or Dutch oven, heat 2 tablespoons of oil over medium-high heat. Add the onions and sauté until soft, about 4 minutes. Add the red bell pepper, turmeric, curry powder, coconut palm sugar, cumin, chili powder, and cinnamon. Cook for 1 to 2 minutes.

2. Add the garlic and cook another minute, then add the curry paste, coconut milk, basil, diced tomatoes, and tomato sauce and continue to cook, stirring occasionally, until the mixture begins to boil. Lower the heat to medium-low and add the bananas and macadamia nuts and cook for 5 to 10 minutes, to allow the flavors to blend.

3. Add the shredded coconut and season with salt and pepper if desired. Serve over rice.

SERVES 4 TO 6

¼ cup canola oil, divided (can substitute grapeseed or olive oil)

2 onions, chopped (about 2½ cups)

1 red bell pepper, chopped

2 teaspoons turmeric

½ teaspoon curry powder (more if you desire)

1 teaspoon coconut palm sugar or maple syrup

2 teaspoons cumin

1 teaspoon chili powder

1 teaspoon cinnamon

4 cloves garlic, minced

2 teaspoons curry paste

1 cup canned coconut milk

¼ cup fresh basil (optional)

1 cup diced fresh tomatoes

8 ounces tomato sauce

2 ripe bananas, sliced into bite-size pieces

1 cup chopped raw macadamia nuts

¼ cup shredded coconut (optional)

1 teaspoon sea salt

¼ to ½ teaspoon pepper

Curried Vegetable Stew

SERVES 8

1 to 2 tablespoons olive oil

1 large onion, finely chopped

2 cups vegetable stock or
    water, divided

3 red potatoes, diced

3 red yams, diced

4 carrots, chopped

1 head cauliflower, cut into
    florets

2 cups chopped green
    beans, cut into 1-inch
    chunks

1 tablespoon minced garlic
    (2 or 3 cloves)

2 teaspoons grated fresh
    ginger

1 (15-ounce) can coconut
    milk

2 teaspoons curry (or more if
    desired)

½ teaspoon turmeric

2 tablespoons red curry
    paste

1 ½ cups peas (fresh if
    possible, but if not,
    organic frozen)

Kosher sea salt to taste

Fresh cracked pepper to
    taste

THIS STEW IS GOOD any time of year, but I like it best during the winter months, as the root vegetables seem to ooze comfort to me. I also love to make this with spring vegetables, such as asparagus, new potatoes, and peas. This stew is great on its own, but served over red or brown rice, it will stretch even further. It stores in the refrigerator for several days and is great left over.

1. Heat a large skillet or Dutch oven to medium-high heat and add the oil. When it is hot, add the onion and sauté until soft, about 4 minutes. Add a small amount of vegetable stock, to avoid sticking, and then add the potatoes, yams, and carrots and sauté another 2 to 3 minutes. Add in the remaining vegetable stock or water and bring to a boil. Turn down the heat and simmer until the potatoes, yams, and carrots are crunchy tender, about 10 to 12 minutes.

2. Add the cauliflower, beans, garlic, ginger, coconut milk, spices, and the curry paste and simmer for 10 to 15 minutes, or until the vegetables are fork tender. Add the peas in the last 5 minutes so that they do not overcook. Add salt and pepper to taste.

3. If you want to thicken the stew, place a few ladles of it in a blender and whirl until thick. Stir back into the stew. Another option is to just smash the potatoes or yams in the pot, to thicken the broth slightly. I don't do either of these on a regular basis, as I like to eat the veggies whole, but feel free to experiment with your stew.

Falafel Patties

MAKES ABOUT
8 PATTIES

2 cups precooked chickpeas
   (or canned if you prefer)
½ cup garbanzo bean flour
6 or 7 cloves garlic, minced
1 cup finely chopped red
   onion
¼ cup chopped fresh parsley
½ cup chopped fresh cilantro
1 tablespoon cumin
¼ to ½ teaspoon cayenne
   pepper
1 teaspoon coriander
¼ to ½ teaspoon sea salt
½ teaspoon fresh cracked
   pepper
Oil for frying

THIS FALAFEL provides you with a ton of protein and it can be served in many ways. For example, serve it as the filling in tacos or formed into a patty as a burger. I love to cook it and then crumble it into salads. Those are just a few ways you can serve it, but I am sure you will think of more!

1. If using dried garbanzo beans, soak and cook according to package directions. If using canned garbanzo beans, drain the beans and rinse with water.

2. Place all the ingredients (except oil for frying) in a food processor and pulse until the mixture is well blended. This will take a minute or so. If the mixture is too thick, add in a small amount of water and pulse until the mixture has a smooth consistency. Remove from the food processor and place in a medium-size bowl and put in the refrigerator for at least 1 hour. **Note:** this can be made up to 24 hours in advance.

3. Take the falafel mixture out of the refrigerator and prepare your patties by taking a small amount of falafel into your clean hands and forming it into a patty about 2 inches in diameter. Place the patty on a platter and then continue to form the rest of the mixture into patties. (If the patties are crumbly, add a small amount of water to ensure they hold together).

4. Heat up to 2 tablespoons of oil in a large skillet over medium-high heat and when hot, add as many of the patties as you can fit into the skillet. Start with less oil and add more if necessary. Cook the patties until they are crispy, about 3 to 4 minutes on each side. Drain on paper towels and continue this process, adding additional oil if needed, until all of the patties are cooked.

Mango Guacamole

MAKES ABOUT 1 CUP

1 medium-size mango, peeled, pitted, and mashed

1 small ripe avocado, peeled, pitted, and mashed

¼ to ⅓ cup chopped fresh cilantro

½ large beefsteak tomato, diced (about ¼ cup)

Squeeze of lime juice (about 1 to 2 tablespoons)

Pinch of cinnamon

Pinch of cumin

Salt and fresh ground pepper (about ¼ teaspoon coarse kosher salt and ¼ teaspoon pepper)

THIS IS AMAZING served alongside the Vegetable Pakoras Fritters (page 162). I would recommend you double the recipe if you are serving a crowd, as it will go quickly! It is also great served as a dip with brown rice chips or served as a topping for nachos or black bean burgers.

1. Mash or chop the mango and avocado and place them in a food processor and pulse until smooth. Add in the cilantro and pulse until blended.

2. Place this mixture in a bowl and stir in the tomato, fresh lime juice, cinnamon, cumin, and salt and pepper to taste. Serve immediately.

Nori Vegetable Rolls

THESE ROLLS ARE very filling, yet not heavy. They are easy to make and fun to eat, and the ingredients can be changed based on your preferences and what's available at your farmers' market (or in your fridge). I love using raw sunflower seeds, but you could also use nuts if you prefer.

1. Soak the sunflower seeds in just enough water to cover them, overnight or at least 4 hours.

2. In a food processor, combine the drained sunflower seeds with the Bragg Liquid Aminos, lemon juice, cilantro, garlic, scallions, and ¼ cup of spinach. Purée the mixture until fully incorporated and smooth.

3. Place a nori sheet on your work surface and begin by placing a layer of spinach leaves (3 or 4) along the edge closest to you. Add a few spoonfuls of the sunflower mixture on top of the spinach, spreading it evenly along the edge. Add slices of carrot, cucumber, and avocado.

4. Carefully and tightly roll the nori sheet into a compact roll. Seal the edge with a dab of warm water and gently fold the ends together. Repeat the process until all 8 rolls are complete, and then slice into bite-size pieces before serving.

MAKES 8 ROLLS

2 cups raw sunflower seeds, soaked at least 4 hours

2 tablespoons Bragg Liquid Aminos

¼ cup lemon juice

¼ cup cilantro

3 teaspoons minced garlic

2 scallions (green onions), white part only

¾ cup chopped spinach, stems removed, divided

8 sheets raw (untoasted) nori

2 carrots, thinly sliced

1 large cucumber, peeled and thinly sliced

1 large avocado, thinly sliced

Spinach and Lentil Enchiladas

SERVES 8

Sauce
¼ cup finely chopped onion
1 teaspoon olive oil
2 tablespoons chili powder
1 teaspoon finely chopped
   garlic
3 cups (28 ounces) fresh
   tomato sauce, or marinara
   sauce
¼ teaspoon cinnamon
   (optional)
¼ teaspoon sea salt
Freshly ground black pepper

Filling
1 ½ cups lentils
1 tablespoon olive oil
¾ cup finely chopped onion
2 tablespoons chopped
   green chiles
1 to 2 teaspoons finely
   chopped garlic
¼ cup chopped sun-dried
   tomatoes (optional)
4 cups chopped fresh
   spinach, stems removed
1 cup water
1 cup vegetable broth
¼ cup red wine (optional)
8 corn tortillas (or brown
   rice)
1 to 2 cups vegan cheddar
   cheese

THESE ENCHILADAS take some time, but they sure are worth the effort. If you like your enchiladas to have a kick to them, add in ½ tablespoon chipotle pepper and cut the chili powder down to 1½ tablespoons. I served these to guests, and they loved the hotter variation. You can serve these with Tofutti Sour Cream, fresh salsa, guacamole, or hummus.

1. Place ½ cup lentils in a large bowl and cover them with water. Let them soak at least 30 minutes and then drain off the water and rinse. While you are soaking the lentils, carry on with the other preparations.

2. Preheat oven to 350°F.

3. To make the sauce, in a saucepan, sauté the onions in olive oil over medium heat until they begin to soften, 3 to 4 minutes. Add the rest of the sauce ingredients and bring to a boil, and then turn off the heat. Set aside.

4. To make the filling, heat a large skillet over medium-high heat and add the oil. When hot, add the onions and sauté 3 to 4 minutes, then add the chiles and cook another 2 to 3 minutes, then add the garlic, stirring occasionally. Cook another minute before adding the sun-dried tomatoes. Sauté 1 to 2 minutes, then add the spinach, soaked lentils, water, vegetable broth, and red wine. Reduce heat to medium and simmer 15 to 20 minutes, or until the lentils are tender.

5. While the filling is cooking, prepare a 9 x 11-inch casserole dish by pouring a ladle full of sauce into the bottom of the dish, spreading to evenly cover the bottom.

6. In a small skillet (do not add oil) soften the tortillas one at a time, over medium heat, swirling around the pan so they do not stick. Flip and heat the other side.

7. Working on a flat work surface, scoop a small amount of the lentil filling into each softened tortilla and roll up lengthwise.

8. Carefully arrange the enchiladas in the baking dish, then completely cover them with the remaining sauce and sprinkle the top with cheddar cheese, if desired. Bake approximately 30 minutes, or until bubbly. Serve hot.

Succotash

SERVES 4

2 cups lima beans, fava beans, butter beans, or cannellini beans

1 tablespoon olive oil

½ cup finely sliced red onion

1 cup sliced carrots

1 cup sliced zucchini, cut into ¼ inch pieces (or 1 cup peeled, chopped eggplant, cut into cubes)

½ to 1 cup chopped red or green bell pepper

1 tablespoon minced garlic

1 large tomato, chopped

¼ to ½ teaspoon dried thyme

1 cup canned coconut milk

2 cups corn, fresh if possible

1 cup peeled, thinly sliced cucumber (optional)

⅛ to ¼ teaspoon cayenne pepper

⅛ teaspoon nutmeg, fresh grated if possible

Pinch of cinnamon

½ teaspoon lemon pepper

1 tablespoon dried cilantro or parsley

½ to ¾ teaspoon sea salt

Pinch of cumin

Fresh cracked pepper to taste

THIS IS A GREAT summertime food. I love white corn, freshly husked, but you can use whatever corn you have on hand, even frozen, if you need to. This dish is slightly spicy, so if you prefer your foods mild, cut out the cayenne pepper. You can use either dried or canned beans.

1. If you are using dried beans, you will need to cook them before adding to this recipe. If that is the case, soak the beans according to package directions, then place the beans in a stockpot and cover completely with water and cook over medium-high heat until the beans are fork tender. If you are using canned beans, drain and rinse the beans.

2. Heat a medium-size skillet to medium-high heat and add a few teaspoons of the olive oil. When hot, add in the onion and sauté until soft, stirring frequently, about 3 to 4 minutes. Add in the carrots and if needed, more of the olive oil and continue to sauté another 2 to 3 minutes. Add in the zucchini (or eggplant) and bell pepper and sauté an additional 3 minutes. Add in the garlic and tomato and cook 1 minute.

3. Add the thyme, coconut milk, corn, cucumber, cayenne pepper, nutmeg, cinnamon, lemon pepper, cilantro or parsley, salt, and cumin and heat through. Season to taste with salt and pepper. This dish stores well in the refrigerator for several days.

Tempeh Tacos

THESE TACOS ARE quick and easy to make. The options for taco shells include: hemp, corn, and brown rice. You can also use a lettuce wrap, with either romaine lettuce or butter lettuce. Top with shredded cabbage, arugula, guacamole, salsa and lime. Put on a sombrero and you might just think you wandered south of the border! Margarita anyone?

1. In a large skillet, heat the olive oil to medium-high. Sauté onions until translucent, then add the bell pepper. Continue to cook 2 to 3 minutes before adding the tempeh and jalapeño pepper. Cook another 2 to 3 minutes, then add the tomatoes, garlic, cilantro, spices, and lime juice, stirring to combine.

2. Reduce heat to medium-low and cook an additional 10 minutes, or until the flavors are blended. Season with salt and pepper to taste.

MAKES 4

1 tablespoon olive oil
1 large onion (about 1 cup chopped)
1 red bell pepper, diced
8 ounces regular tempeh, cut into 1-inch chunks
1 tablespoon chopped jalapeño pepper
1 cup chopped fresh tomato
3 cloves garlic, minced
¼ cup chopped fresh cilantro
2 teaspoons chili powder
1 teaspoon cumin
½ teaspoon cayenne pepper
¼ teaspoon cinnamon
2 tablespoons lime juice
½ teaspoon kosher salt
Freshly ground black pepper
4 taco shells

Traditional Vegetable Lasagna

SERVES 6 TO 8

Sauce

2½ cups tomato sauce

½ cup tomato paste

¼ cup red wine (a full-bodied
  Cabernet is good in this
  recipe)

2 bay leaves

½ to 1 teaspoon minced
  garlic

3 tablespoons chopped fresh
  basil

¼ cup chopped fresh parsley

1 teaspoon dried oregano

½ teaspoon fresh cracked
  pepper

(continues)

WHAT I LOVE about lasagna is that you can add in any vegetables you have left over and it will turn out great. If you don't have any broccoli in the house but you feel like making veggie lasagna, substitute fresh peas, red bell peppers, cauliflower, or whatever else you might have on hand.

1. In a medium-size bowl, combine the sauce ingredients. Stir well and then set aside for at least 30 minutes or longer to allow the flavors to blend.

2. Lightly steam the following vegetables: broccoli, carrots, spinach, and zucchini. (We are going to bake this dish, so don't oversteam the veggies to where they turn to mush!)

3. In a large skillet, heat 1 tablespoon of the olive oil over medium-high heat, and when hot, add the onions. Sauté for about 4 minutes, or until soft and translucent. Add in the mushrooms and continue to cook until the juices begin to run from the mushrooms and they begin to turn brown, about 4 or 5 minutes. Add in the wine and mock cream cheese. This mixture will be thick, so be careful not to overcook it as we don't want it to get too thick! Turn off the heat.

4. Preheat oven to 350°F.

5. Remove the bay leaves from the tomato sauce and pour about 1 ½ cups of the sauce into the bottom of a 13 x 9 x 2-inch dish. Spread it out over the entire bottom of the dish. Then add 3 full lengths of the drained lasagna noodles on top of the sauce. Layer some of the steamed vegetables over the top of the noodles and then dollop the onion-mushroom mixture on top. (If the onion-mushroom mixture is too thick, you can thin it slightly by adding in some vegetable broth or a touch more wine.) Sprinkle some of the grated cheese over the vegetables, then more sauce, and continue this process until you have used up all of the ingredients.

6. Sprinkle some cheese on the top and then bake for about 45 minutes, or until the lasagna is cooked through and the cheese is bubbly. Serve hot. This dish reheats well either on the stovetop or in the microwave. It stores well in the refrigerator for several days and freezes well, too.

Lasagna Filling

2 cups sliced broccoli, cut lengthwise into strips

1 cup sliced carrots, sliced into strips

1 cup chopped spinach, stems removed

1 cup sliced zucchini

1 tablespoon plus 1 teaspoon olive oil, divided

1 cup chopped onion

2 cups cleaned, sliced mushrooms, stems removed

2 tablespoons red wine, Cabernet or Zinfandel (or veggie broth if you prefer)

½ cup Tofutti cream cheese

8 gluten-free lasagna noodles (such as Tinkyada brown rice noodles), cooked according to package directions and drained

2 cups grated vegan mozzarella cheese (Follow Your Heart brand works well)

Vegetable Pakoras Fritters

SERVES 4

1 teaspoon sea salt

½ teaspoon ground
   coriander

½ teaspoon ground turmeric

½ teaspoon chili powder

½ teaspoon garam masala

1 cup garbanzo bean flour

2 cloves garlic, minced

1 to 1 ¼ cups water

½ head eggplant (peeled
   and chopped into cubes),
   1 small chopped zucchini,
   or 1 cup chopped broccoli
   florets (bite-size pieces)

1 large onion, peeled and
   cut into rings **or** 1 cup
   mushrooms, cleaned and
   stems removed

¼ to ½ cup canola oil **or**
   grapeseed oil for frying

I HAVE PROVIDED a variety of vegetables that you can use in this recipe, but there are others. Green beans work well with this dish as do thinly sliced yams and zucchini. I like to serve this dish with hummus or mango chutney, but you can also serve it with a peanut sauce.

Note: My recipe tester Kristine does not fry any foods, so she dipped the vegetables in the batter and then placed them on a cookie sheet. She baked them in the oven at 350ºF for 20 minutes and said they were wonderful. So, if you wish to reduce the oil in your diet, dip and bake!

1. In a large bowl, combine the sea salt and spices with the garbanzo flour. Add the garlic and stir. Slowly add the water to the flour mixture and stir with a whisk until the batter is blended. Do not add all of the water at once; you want to add in part of the water, whisk it together with the flour and then add a bit more, until you achieve the right consistency (not too thin or thick, so the vegetables will hold the batter when dipped into it).

2. Heat a Dutch oven or other deep saucepan or wok over nearly high heat. Add about 1½ inches of oil. When it is hot, dip the vegetables into the batter and then drop into the oil, cooking until browned. The timing will depend on what vegetables you are cooking. The onions cook very quickly, but the cauliflower and broccoli will take longer. The mushrooms will release their juices when they are cooked. Stay next to the stove and flip the vegetables around so they brown on all sides. Drain on paper towels. Continue this process until all of the vegetables are cooked. It is important that you have the heat high enough so the vegetables cook quickly and do not absorb too much of the oil.

Delightful Desserts

Apple Pie

WHAT ISN'T COMFORTING about apple pie? Come on, this is America! I couldn't write a cookbook and not include this recipe. I found that using organic coconut oil in the piecrust gives the apple pie a very unique and delicious flavor. This recipe calls for organic sugar, but you can easily substitute organic maple syrup. You will have a slightly juicer pie because of the liquid in the syrup, but who cares really? It tastes good! This can be served with coconut milk ice cream.

1. Preheat the oven to 350°F. Prepare the crusts.

2. Place the apples in a large bowl and add the arrowroot, tapioca, cinnamon, salt, and sugar. Stir this mixture together really well and toss the apples to coat them with the mixture.

3. Carefully arrange the apple slices in the bottom piecrust and then gently cover the apples with the top crust. Pinch the edges of the crusts together and then cut small incisions in the top crust to let steam escape, before putting the pie in the oven.

4. Bake for 50 to 60 minutes, or until the apples are bubbly and the top crust is lightly browned. If the top crust becomes too dark, cover lightly with recycled aluminum foil.

5. Cool on a wire rack.

SERVES 8

Two-Crust Piecrust (page 184)

6 cored, thinly sliced cups apples (peeled if desired)

1 tablespoon arrowroot powder

1 tablespoon tapioca powder

1 heaping teaspoon cinnamon

Pinch of sea salt

⅔ cup organic sugar

Banana Cream Pie

SERVES 8

1 prebaked piecrust

3 ripe bananas, mashed (approximately 1¼ cups)

1 cup peeled and chopped yam (precooked)

Pinch of salt

1 tablespoon lemon or lime juice

¼ cup So Delicious coconut milk (or soy or hemp milk)

¼ cup agave nectar or maple syrup

2 teaspoons vanilla

MimicCreme Healthy Top whipping cream (or other nondairy whipped topping)

BANANA CREAM PIE is already lots of fun, so why not yam it up? This will be your family's new favorite, especially if you can find a soy-based whipped topping at the grocery store. If you don't eat soy, I am thrilled to report there's Healthy Top whipping cream from MimicCreme is made from cashews, almonds, and coconut. It whips up like the "real deal," and it tastes delicious! I recommend you use the Nutty Piecrust from page 183 as your base; it goes amazingly well with the yams.

1. Thoroughly mash the bananas until completely smooth. Place bananas, yam, and salt into a food processor and pulse until a rich, smooth consistency is achieved. Add lemon juice, coconut milk, agave nectar or maple syrup, and vanilla and continue pulsing until all of the ingredients are well combined.

2. Pour mixture into premade piecrust and refrigerate for at least 1 to 2 hours.

3. Before serving, cover the pie with slices of banana (additional) and whipped topping.

Note: You can also use a Raw Pie Crust in this recipe, if you prefer.

Cashew Cheesecake

THIS CHEESECAKE will bring a smile to your face! It is easy to make; it rivals any dairy-filled cheesecake; and topped with a fresh berry compote, it makes a fabulous dessert to serve your family and friends!

1. Put cashews in a food processor and pulse until finely ground. Add the maple syrup, dates, palm shortening, lemon juice, and vanilla bean seeds. Whirl until smooth.

2. When the filling is completely blended, transfer to a prebaked or raw piecrust and let set in the refrigerator for at least 1 hour. Top with fresh berries, peaches, plums, or whatever fruit you wish.

SERVES 8

1 prebaked or raw piecrust

3 cups raw cashews

½ cup maple syrup or agave nectar

4 tablespoons pitted and chopped Medjool dates

½ cup melted palm shortening (or coconut oil)

½ cup lemon juice

1 vanilla bean (seeds only)

Fresh fruit as desired

Chocolate Chip–Oatmeal Cookies

1 cup buttery spread (vegan margarine), Spectrum or a combination of organic virgin coconut oil

½ cup pure maple syrup

½ cup organic sugar

2 tablespoons warm water

1 ½ teaspoons Ener-G egg replacer

1 teaspoon vanilla

1 cup brown rice flour

1 cup sorghum flour

¼ cup coconut flour

2 teaspoons baking powder

1 teaspoon baking soda

½ to 1 teaspoon salt

1 teaspoon cinnamon

2 cups gluten-free oats

1 cup chopped walnuts

1 cup Enjoy Life Foods vegan chocolate chips

THESE CHOCOLATE chip–oatmeal cookies are great whether they're eaten right out of the oven or several days later. They are not crumbly, and you would never know they are gluten-free! Be sure to store them in an airtight container. If you are into chia seeds, try replacing the powdered egg replacer and water with 1 teaspoon chia seeds mixed with 2 tablespoons water. Let the chia seeds sit in the water for 5 to 10 minutes, until the mixture becomes gooey or thick, and then add to the wet ingredients.

1. Preheat the oven to 350°F. Line a cookie sheet with parchment paper.

2. In a mixer, beat together the buttery spread, maple syrup, and sugar until well blended. This mixture will look quite fluffy. In a small bowl, whisk together the warm water and egg replacer until bubbly and well blended. Add to the wet ingredients. Add the vanilla and continue blending.

3. In another bowl, add the flours, baking powder, baking soda, salt, and cinnamon. Stir until well blended and add to the wet ingredients. Blend well. Add the oats and walnuts and continue to stir together; the mixture will be thick. Add in the chocolate chips and stir by hand until mixed well.

4. Drop the dough onto the prepared cookie sheet in tablespoonfuls, placing 3 cookies per row. Flatten each cookie out and bake for 15 to 17 minutes. Oven heats vary, so check the cookies sooner if you think your oven runs hot. The cookie tops will not be very brown, but the bottoms will be a golden color when they are done. Cool on wire racks. These cookies are really hearty. They should be solid and about ⅛ inch thick.

5. Enjoy. Store in an airtight container.

Chocolate–Dried Cherry Biscotti

1⅓ cups almond flour

1 cup almond meal

2 tablespoons arrowroot powder

¼ cup organic cocoa powder (I use Now brand)

1 tablespoon finely ground decaf coffee

¾ teaspoon baking soda

¼ teaspoon sea salt

½ cup chopped walnuts or pecans

¼ cup finely chopped dried cherries

½ cup vegan chocolate chips (I use Enjoy Life Foods brand)

½ cup organic maple syrup

1 tablespoon water

This recipe came from my dear friend Barbara who lives in New York. Her recipe did not include dried cherries or walnuts, but I find these additions really tip this recipe over the edge! These biscotti are more like a fudgy brownie than a traditional biscotti, and the trick is to get to the second baking! Almond flour is very expensive, so if you prefer, just use all almond meal. You can find it at Trader Joe's for a very reasonable price.

1. Preheat the oven to 350°F. Line a cookie sheet with parchment paper.

2. In a large bowl, combine the almond flour, almond meal, arrowroot, cocoa, ground coffee, baking soda, and sea salt. Stir to mix together. Add in the walnuts, dried cherries, chocolate chips, maple syrup, and water. Stir this mixture together really well. The batter will be sticky.

3. Using clean hands, mold the batter into two logs about 6 to 7 inches long and about 1 ½ to 2 inches thick.

4. Cut each log into diagonal slices. Carefully pick up each slice and transfer to the prepared cookie sheet. Bake the biscotti for 15 minutes and then cool on a wire rack for about 1 hour.

5. Preheat the oven to 300°F and return the biscotti to the oven to bake another 10 minutes. Turn the biscotti over and bake another 5 to 10 minutes on the other side.

6. Cool on a wire rack. These won't last long, but if they do, store them in an airtight container.

Chocolate, Dried Cherry, and Walnut Fudge

**MAKES ABOUT
24 PIECES**

⅔ cup So Delicious coconut
milk (or soy or hemp milk)

1 ¼ cups organic sugar

¼ cup vegan margarine

1 ½ cups chocolate chips
(Enjoy Life Foods or other
vegan brand)

½ cup chopped raw walnuts

½ cup chopped dried
cherries

1 teaspoon vanilla

I SURVEYED LOTS OF PEOPLE on their favorite "comfort foods" and many said FUDGE. This fudge never lasts long when I make it. I have tested it on at least twenty people and they all loved it—I hope you will too. Remember, everything in moderation!

1. Line an 8 x 8-inch square pan with waxed paper.

2. Combine the coconut milk, sugar, and margarine in a heavy saucepan and cook over medium heat until the mixture comes to a boil. Maintain the boil for 5 minutes, then immediately remove from the heat and stir in the chocolate chips, walnuts, dried cherries, and vanilla.

3. Pour the mixture into the prepared pan and spread it out evenly. Place in the refrigerator until it sets, at least 2 to 3 hours. When the mixture is hard, lift the waxed paper out of the pan and set on a work surface. Peel off the paper and cut into 1-inch squares.

4. Store in an airtight container.

Chocolate, Zucchini, and Apple Bread

I SENT THIS BREAD to a recipe tester by the name of Kristine. I had met Kristine by chance, and I am so glad we met, as she is the best recipe tester I have ever worked with. She gave this recipe an A+. I also shared this with several taste testers and every one of them said they couldn't believe it was gluten-free and egg-free!

The all-purpose flour works well in this recipe, but you can also substitute sorghum flour if desired.

1. Preheat oven to 350°F. Grease 2 bread pans with canola oil and then dust with flour. Brush off any extra flour.

2. In a large bowl, stir together all of the dry ingredients until well mixed. Set aside.

3. In a mixer bowl, combine the coconut oil, canola oil, maple syrup, and sugar until well blended and fluffy. (Start out on low, scraping down the sides of the bowl, and then mix on high for a minute or so). Add in the egg replacer and water mixture, coconut milk, applesauce, and vanilla and stir well to incorporate. Add in the zucchini, apple, and nuts and stir.

4. Slowly add the dry ingredients to the wet ingredients and mix until well incorporated.

(continues)

MAKES 2 LOAVES

2 cups all-purpose gluten-free flour (Bob's Red Mill works great for this recipe)

½ cup brown rice flour

¼ cup coconut flour

½ cup cocoa powder

2 teaspoons baking powder

2 teaspoons baking soda

¾ teaspoon salt (you may use less if you prefer)

1 heaping teaspoon cinnamon

1 teaspoon guar gum (or xanthan gum)

½ cup coconut oil

¼ cup canola oil

½ cup organic maple syrup

1 cup organic sugar or organic coconut palm sugar

1 ½ teaspoons Ener-G egg replacer whisked together well with 2 tablespoons warm water (until frothy)

½ cup So Delicious coconut milk (not canned; or soy or hemp milk)

Chocolate, Zucchini, and Apple Bread *(continued)*

½ cup chunky applesauce (to reduce the fat, omit the canola oil and add ¼ cup more applesauce)

1½ teaspoons vanilla

2 cups grated zucchini

1 cup grated apple (tart apple works best)

½ cup chopped walnuts or pecans

5. Pour half of the batter into each prepared bread pan and then place on the center rack of the oven and bake for about 45 minutes.

6. Check each loaf for doneness at 40 minutes with a toothpick. It should come out clean when inserted in the center of the bread. If it is not done, continue to bake until a toothpick or sharp knife comes out clean. Cool on a wire rack for about 10 minutes and then remove from the pans and continue to cool.

Coconut–Black Rice Pudding

I HAVE A FAVORITE restaurant near where I live, and they make the best black rice pudding on the planet. I don't know what their secret ingredient is, but this is as close as I can get to theirs. You can add a bit of vanilla to this recipe too, if you want to change it up a bit. You can also add chopped Medjool dates, chopped walnuts, or raisins.

1. Place the rice and coconut milks in a saucepan and cook over medium-low heat for approximately 1 hour, or until the mixture is thickened and the rice is fully cooked.

2. Add in the maple syrup, candied ginger, and spices and stir until well incorporated. Cook over medium-low heat for approximately 1 hour, or until the pudding is thickened, stirring occasionally.

SERVES 4

1 cup black rice, washed

1 (14-ounce) can coconut milk

1 cup So Delicious coconut milk

2 tablespoons to ¼ cup maple syrup

1½ tablespoons chopped candied ginger

½ teaspoon cinnamon

¼ teaspoon cardamom

Hawaiian Pudding

SERVES 4

4 ripe avocados, peeled and
    pit removed
2 ripe bananas
2 large papayas, with fruit
    scooped out of the skins
2 tablespoons lime juice
½ fresh pineapple
¼ cup toasted unsweetened
    coconut (optional)

I WAS RECENTLY visiting Kauai, where the fresh fruits listed in this recipe are found all over the island. No wonder the folks who live there have such beautiful skin—they eat fresh papayas, bananas, and avocados all year long. You will need to be adventurous when you make this, as the serving "dish" is half of a pineapple. It's so delicious you may need to double the recipe!

1. Mash the avocados, bananas, and papayas really well on a plate or in a bowl and then add in the lime juice.

2. Cut a pineapple in half and cut out the core. Cut away the pineapple from the sides of the fruit, making a "boat" in the middle. Cut the useable pineapple into chunks and add to the mashed fruit.

3. Pour the pudding mixture into the pineapple and sprinkle toasted coconut on top, if desired. Get out the forks and dig in!

Heavenly Raw Pumpkin Pie

THIS PIE TAKES very little time to make. The filling is raw, but the piecrust I recommend is cooked. If you prefer to stick with all raw, then use the Raw Piecrust recipe found on page 188. My taste testers loved this pie and couldn't believe it didn't have any dairy in it.

1. Combine all of the filling ingredients except the pumpkin in a food processor and purée until smooth. When the nuts and dates are smooth and creamy, add in the pumpkin and pulse until the mixture is fully incorporated and nice and smooth.

2. Pour the filling into the prepared crust and serve, or refrigerate up to a day ahead. You can store it for 2 to 3 days in an airtight container in the refrigerator.

MAKES ENOUGH FILLING FOR ONE 8-INCH PIE

Nutty Piecrust (page 183), cooked and completely cooled

½ cup raw macadamia nuts

½ cup raw cashews

¼ cup pitted Medjool dates

3 tablespoons maple syrup

⅛ cup ground or flaked coconut

¾ teaspoon cinnamon

¼ teaspoon nutmeg

⅛ teaspoon ground ginger

3½ cups canned or fresh organic pumpkin

Key Lime Pie

SERVES 8

Nutty Piecrust (page 183), cooked and completely cooled (optional)

2 tablespoons ground cashews

2 packages Nori extra firm tofu, drained

¾ cup Follow Your Heart sour cream

¾ cup organic coconut palm sugar

2 tablespoons maple syrup

½ cup organic lime juice or fresh-squeezed limes

1 teaspoon grated lime zest, to garnish

I WANTED TO make a pie filling that would be scrumptious and refreshing all at the same time. The combination of lime and maple syrup really works well in this recipe. It is so easy to make and the rewards are great. I have served this only as a pie, but you could skip the crust and serve this as a pudding in parfait dishes with cookies crumbled over the top if you prefer.

1. Start by placing the cashews in the food processor and then pulse until they are ground. Add in all the other ingredients except the lime zest and pulse until really well blended. The mixture should be very creamy and smooth. If lumps are present, pulse for another minute or until it is smooth.

2. Pour the mixture into a prepared pie shell and sprinkle the pie with lime zest, or pour into bowls if serving as a pudding. Refrigerate for at least an hour before serving. Enjoy!

Lavender-Lemon Shortbread

LAVENDER isn't just for bedtime! Cooking with lavender buds can delight your taste buds and turn your kitchen into an English garden. In fact, you might consider planting lavender in your garden if you don't currently have it, as it is truly a versatile herb. Lavender is one of the ingredients in herbes de Provence, an herbal blend that I often use in cooking.

1. Preheat the oven to 350°F and lightly spray or grease a 9-inch springform pan with canola oil.

2. In a large bowl, cream together the buttery spread and both sugars. Add in the lemon juice and beat well to fully incorporate.

3. In a separate bowl, sift together the flours, salt, and lavender buds. **Note:** I like to see the lavender buds in the shortbread, so I put some into the flour mixture. You don't have to include it if you don't want to, but it's quite lovely.

4. Add the dry ingredients to the wet and beat on low speed with a mixer until well blended. You will need to scrape down the sides of the bowl a few times.

5. Transfer the shortbread mixture into the prepared pan and press until it is firmly packed down. Prick the mixture with a fork in several places so that air can escape during the baking process.

6. Bake for 20 to 25 minutes, or until the shortbread is lightly browned. Cool on a wire rack before cutting. Cut into 12 equal pieces.

MAKES 12 PIECES

¾ cup plus 1 tablespoon nondairy buttery spread (Earth Balance is the brand I use)

½ cup organic sugar

2 tablespoons organic brown sugar

1 tablespoon lemon juice (fresh is best)

½ cup coconut flour

½ cup brown rice flour

1 cup sorghum flour

1 tablespoon English lavender buds

Pinch of salt

½ teaspoon guar gum or xanthan gum

Molasses Cookies

¾ cup palm shortening

1 cup organic sugar

1 tablespoon maple syrup

1½ teaspoons Ener-G egg replacer whisked together really well with 2 table-spoons warm water (or 1 teaspoon chia seeds mixed together with 2 tablespoons water; let sit for up to 10 minutes)

¼ cup blackstrap molasses

2 cups sorghum flour

2 tablespoons coconut flour

2 teaspoons baking soda

1 teaspoon cinnamon

½ teaspoon ginger

½ teaspoon cloves

½ teaspoon sea salt

MY MOM was known for her molasses cookies. My kids used to ask me all the time to make grandma's version of these cookies, but after I came up with this recipe, they stopped asking for hers. I also tried these out on the neighborhood kids, none of whom are either gluten-free or vegan, and they all came running over asking for more. I think they are a keeper!

1. Preheat the oven to 375°F. Line a cookie sheet with parchment paper.

2. In a small saucepan, heat the shortening over medium-low heat until it is melted, then let cool completely.

3. Place the cooled shortening in a large mixing bowl and add the sugar, maple syrup, egg replacer, and molasses. Beat on high to mix together well. Scrape down the sides of the bowl and then add in the flours, baking soda, spices, and sea salt. Mix well to fully incorporate the dry ingredients with the wet.

4. Roll the cookie dough by tablespoons onto the prepared cookie sheet. Bake for 10 to 12 minutes. Cool on wire rack. Store in an airtight container.

Nutty Piecrust

A NUTTY CRUST for the rest of us! This is a great all-around crust, excellent for sweet and savory pies alike. Whether you would like a traditional dessert or a new take on a classic quiche, this versatile little crust has you covered!

1. Preheat the oven to 350°F.

2. Combine the walnuts, pecans, almond meal, brown rice flour, cinnamon, and sea salt in a food processor. Pulse until mixture is finely ground. Add in the maple syrup or agave cactus nectar and mix well. Transfer the mixture into a large bowl and cut in the palm shortening with a pastry cutter or fork. This is a very important step, as you need to fully incorporate the shortening into the nut mixture. Take your time and be sure it's completely mixed in.

3. Press this mixture into a 9-inch pie dish and push along the bottom and up the sides until it is evenly spread over the pie shell. Another very important step is to prick the crust all over with a fork before baking. This will prevent any air from being trapped under the crust. Be sure you also prick the sides as well as the bottom of the crust.

4. Bake for 15 to 18 minutes or until the edges are browned and the crust is cooked through. Cool on a wire rack.

MAKES ONE 9-INCH CRUST

1 cup walnuts
1 cup pecans
½ cup almond meal
¼ cup brown rice flour
½ teaspoon cinnamon
½ teaspoon sea salt
¼ cup maple syrup or agave nectar
¼ cup palm shortening or organic virgin coconut oil

Two-Crust Piecrust

3 cups sorghum flour (or
    2 cups sorghum flour and
    1 cup brown rice flour)
¼ cup organic sugar
¼ teaspoon sea salt
1½ cups organic coconut oil
    (or a combination of
    coconut oil, palm
    shortening, and/or vegan
    margarine)
6 to 7 tablespoons cold
    water
1 tablespoon white vinegar

THE FLAVOR OF THIS CRUST is really amazing. I highly recommend you use organic coconut oil if you can, because the flavor it imparts is just wonderful. The other great thing about this crust is it really browns up nicely and has a special crunch to it. The downside, of course, is that there is a lot of fat in this piecrust recipe. I think you could cut the shortening to 1 cup and it would work, but it will not have the same texture. If you are concerned about the amount of fat used, consider using less shortening and more water to hold this crust together.

1. Preheat the oven to 350°F. Lightly spray a 9-inch pie pan with canola oil.

2. In a large bowl, combine the flour, sugar, and sea salt and stir to blend. Cut in the organic coconut oil with a pastry cutter or fork. This takes some time, as you really need to work with the coconut oil or palm shortening to incorporate it into the flour mixture.

3. Once you have the coconut oil fully incorporated, add the water and vinegar together in a separate bowl then slowly pour it into the flour mixture. Don't add all 6 or 7 tablespoons at once, or it may make your dough too wet. I recommend you add in 5 or 6 tablespoons, work the dough to bring it together, and if that isn't enough water, then add another tablespoon until you achieve the right texture. I found I needed 7 tablespoons of water to make this dough come together nicely. You want to be able to use your hands to form the dough into one big ball.

4. I use waxed paper to roll the dough out on, so tear off two good-size pieces of waxed paper and place one on your work surface.

5. Break the large ball into 2 smaller ones and press the first ball between 2 large pieces of waxed paper and then roll out into a large circle. Be careful not to roll the dough too thin, or it will tear when you try to shape it into the pie dish.

6. Slowly pull the top piece of waxed paper off the pie dough and carefully flip the pie dough into the pie dish. Once you have it in the pie dish, slowly and carefully lift the second piece of waxed paper from the pie dough and then form the pie shell into the pie dish.

7. Add your pie filling and then repeat this process to roll the dough for the top crust. Place the top crust over the filling and then seal the edges. Cut off any dough that remains around the edges and bake until done.

Pineapple Upside-Down Cake

SERVES 8

¼ cup palm shortening or
vegan margarine

½ cup organic brown sugar

1 (14-ounce) can of sliced
pineapple or 1 fresh
pineapple

Fresh or dried cherries
(optional)

1½ teaspoons Ener-G egg
replacer

2 tablespoons water

¾ cup organic maple syrup

¾ cup So Delicious coconut
milk (not canned), or other
milk of your choice

½ teaspoon vanilla

2 cups sorghum flour

2 teaspoons baking powder

1 teaspoon guar gum or
xanthan gum

FRESH PINEAPPLE upside-down cake is such a treat! I first came up with this recipe when I was visiting Kauai, my favorite place on the planet. If you are using a fresh pineapple you can either cut away the outer skin of the pineapple, core it, and then cut it into rings, or you can take the easy way out as I do and just slice the pineapple lengthwise, until you have enough slices to completely cover the bottom of the skillet. Do not cut the slices too thin—about a quarter inch is what you need. If you are using canned pineapple, buy a 14-ounce can and drain the slices before arranging them over the brown sugar mixture. Finally, I recommend using a cast iron skillet, but if you don't have one, you can bake this in a pie dish.

1. Preheat the oven to 350°F.

2. Heat the cast iron skillet over medium heat and add the palm shortening or margarine. When it has melted, sprinkle the brown sugar over the top. Arrange the pineapple slices over the top of the brown sugar and set aside. Be sure to cover as much of the skillet as possible. You can put a cherry or dried cherries in the centers of the pineapple rings if you wish.

3. In a medium-size bowl, whisk together the egg replacer with 2 tablespoons of warm water until the mixture is very bubbly. Add in the maple syrup, coconut milk, vanilla, sorghum flour, baking powder, and guar gum and beat until well incorporated, about 3 to 4 minutes. Scrape down the sides of the bowl and stir together well. Pour this mixture over the top of the pineapple and bake for 40 minutes or until a toothpick inserted in the center comes out clean.

4. As soon as you remove the skillet from the oven, flip it over onto a serving platter that is big enough to center the cake. Carefully remove the skillet, making sure none of the pineapple has stuck to the bottom. If it has, carefully remove any pineapple using a knife and lay it out where it should go on the cake. If there is any juice left in the bottom of the pan, drizzle it over the top of the pineapple. Cool on a wire rack.

Raw Piecrust

1 cup raw macadamia nuts

2 cups raw walnuts

1 cup pitted Medjool dates

1 teaspoon cinnamon

¼ teaspoon sea salt

1 tablespoon agave nectar

YUMMY. No other word describes a crust like this one. You can serve this with the Key Lime Pie filling on page 180 or the Pineapple and Strawberry Smoothie Pie filling on page 189. It is a good idea to chill this pie shell before serving, so it will stick together with your filling.

1. Place all the ingredients in a food processor and pulse until the mixture is finely ground and fully blended. Press this mixture into a pie shell and press it up the sides evenly. Fill with your favorite filling and enjoy!

Raw Pineapple and Strawberry Smoothie Pie

HOW ABOUT EATING your smoothie instead of drinking it? This pie will delight everyone in the family. One of the best things about it is that it takes only minutes to make, and everything in it is raw, as nature intended! So, dig in and enjoy.

1. Place all the ingredients except the sesame seeds in a food processor and pulse until completely smooth. Pour into a raw piecrust and sprinkle the sesame seeds on top.

SERVES 8

1 Raw Piecrust (page 188)
2 cups chopped pineapple
2 cups fresh strawberries, de-stemmed
¾ cup mashed banana
½ cup pitted and chopped Medjool dates
2 tablespoons coconut flour (or almond meal or flaxmeal)
3 tablespoons fresh-squeezed orange juice
½ teaspoon cinnamon
½ cup sesame seeds

Toffee Bars

MAKES 24 BARS

½ cup vegan margarine

½ cup virgin coconut oil

2 tablespoons cashew butter
(or peanut butter or
almond butter)

1 teaspoon vanilla

1 cup organic brown sugar

1 cup brown rice flour

1 cup sorghum flour

½ teaspoon sea salt

1½ teaspoon guar gum or
xanthan gum

½ cup finely chopped raw
walnuts

1 cup vegan chocolate chips

I TESTED THESE toffee bars out on my neighbors who all loved them! I knew these were a hit when the kids asked for more. These are great as a holiday cookie or just as an anytime bar to take to a cookout.

1. Preheat the oven to 350°F.

2. In a large mixing bowl, combine the margarine, coconut oil, cashew butter, vanilla, and brown sugar and beat together well. Scrape down the sides of the bowl with a spatula and add in the flours, sea salt, and guar gum.

3. Pour this mixture into a 9 x 9-inch square pan and bake for 20 to 25 minutes, or until the toffee bars are lightly browned and not too doughy in the middle. As soon as they are done, remove from the oven and immediately sprinkle with the nuts and chocolate chips.

4. Cool on a wire rack until slightly cool. When the bars are cool enough to touch, but NOT cold, using clean hands, press slightly on the chocolate chips and walnuts to "set" them into the bars, so the top layer stays with the bottom of the bar when you cut it. When completely cool, cut into 24 bars. Store in an airtight container.

Strawberry Shortcake

SPRING IS A TIME for eating fresh, organic strawberries. I put them in my smoothies, salads, and yes, of course, I make homemade strawberry shortcake too! Who can resist? With nondairy whipped topping, I think I've gone to strawberry heaven.

1. Preheat the oven to 425°F. Lightly spray a 9-inch pie dish with canola oil.

2. Place all the dry ingredients (flours, baking powder, sea salt, and guar gum) in a large bowl and cut in the coconut oil until well combined. In a small bowl, combine the coconut milk and 2 table-spoons maple syrup and add to the dry ingredients.

3. Scoop the batter into the prepared pie dish and spread until evenly distributed. Bake for about 15 minutes, or until a toothpick or knife inserted in the center comes out clean. Cool on a wire rack.

4. Clean the strawberries, slice them, and place them in a bowl and drizzle about 1 to 2 teaspoons maple syrup over the top. Cover and place in the refrigerator until ready to eat.

5. Before using the mock whipped cream, place it in the refrigerator for at least 1 hour. Whip it according to package directions.

(continues)

SERVES 6 TO 8

1 cup brown rice flour

1 cup sorghum flour

4 teaspoons baking powder

1 teaspoon sea salt

1 teaspoon guar gum

1/3 cup extra virgin coconut oil

1 cup So Delicious coconut milk

2 tablespoons plus 1 to 2 teaspoons organic maple syrup (for a sweeter shortcake, double the syrup you add to the cake)

2 pints fresh, organic strawberries

1 carton Healthy Top whipping cream (MimicCreme, made from cashews, almonds, and coconut)

Mint leaves, for garnish (optional)

Strawberry Shortcake *(continued)*

6. To serve, cut a wedge of the shortcake and slice it in half lengthwise. Place one slice of shortbread on a serving dish and dollop some of the whipped topping over the top. Spoon a generous heaping of strawberries on top of the whipped topping, then top with the other half of the shortbread and add another heaping of the whipped topping. You can garnish with mint leaves if desired.

Peach Ice Cream

YOU WILL NEED an ice cream maker for this recipe. I use a Mini Hamilton Beach ice cream maker, which takes only about 20 minutes to make a pint of ice cream. Coconut milk ice cream rivals any dairy version in my humble opinion! Feel free to change up the fruit in this recipe. It is also great with raspberries, marionberries, and bananas.

1. Place all of the ingredients in the ice cream maker and follow the manufacturer's directions. As I said, I have a Hamilton Beach ice cream machine and it works fabulously; the ice cream stores in the freezer in the dish it is made in, and it is super easy to clean.

1 PINT

1 cup mashed peaches

⅓ cup canned coconut milk (or So Delicious, but it's not as creamy)

½ teaspoon vanilla

3 tablespoons coconut palm sugar (or organic sugar or organic maple syrup)

¼ teaspoon cinnamon

Everything Else

Avocado Mayo

AVOCADO IS nature's butter, only better! This tangy spread breathes new life into sandwiches and wraps topped with hummus, cucumbers, sprouts, and bell peppers. You can say farewell to the same ol' mayo!

1. Place everything into a food processor and purée until mayonnaise consistency is achieved. Season to taste. This stores well in the fridge if you keep the avocado pit in the mixture. It won't likely last long!

MAKES ABOUT 1 CUP

2 avocados

3 to 4 tablespoons Vegenaise

3 tablespoons lemon or lime juice

¼ teaspoon hot sauce

¼ teaspoon chipotle pepper

Salt and pepper

Balsamic Vinaigrette Dressing

MAKES ABOUT ⅔ CUP

2 tablespoons balsamic
vinegar

1 tablespoon red wine

1 tablespoon fresh lemon
juice

1 teaspoon gluten-free
tamari

1 tablespoon agave nectar

¼ cup extra virgin olive oil

¼ teaspoon dried tarragon

¼ teaspoon dried oregano

1 teaspoon chopped fresh
basil

Pinch of salt and pepper to
taste

MY COUSIN KIMI gave me this recipe many years ago. We lost her to cancer last year, and every time I make it, I think of her smiling face. You can double the recipe if you wish and keep whatever you don't use in a jar in the refrigerator. It will last for several weeks.

1. Place all of the ingredients in a glass jar. Place the lid on firmly and shake briskly for a minute or so, until the mixture is well blended. Use to dress your salad as desired. Refrigerate leftover dressing in jar.

Peanut Sauce

THIS PEANUT SAUCE is great served over spinach and red rice (Lundberg Family Farms) or any veggies. I also love it served over noodles, Pad Thai–style. It is not too spicy, so if you want more of a kick, feel free to add more curry paste or red pepper flakes, or add cayenne pepper to it.

1. Place all of the ingredients in a blender and purée until well blended. If serving over veggies or noodles, heat before serving.

MAKES ABOUT 1 CUP

½ cup peanut butter (smooth)

¼ teaspoon green curry paste

2 tablespoons gluten-free tamari

½ cup water

1 teaspoon apple cider vinegar

2 tablespoons organic brown sugar

2 tablespoons coconut milk

2 tablespoons sesame tahini

Dash of red pepper flakes

Pesto Sauce

2 cups chopped Italian
   parsley

1 cup chopped fresh basil

⅓ cup plus 1 tablespoon
   extra virgin olive oil

⅓ cup pine nuts

¼ to ½ teaspoon minced
   garlic

¼ cup white wine or
   vegetable broth

1 teaspoon dried oregano

½ cup sun-dried tomatoes

¼ to ½ cup vegetable broth

THIS PESTO SAUCE can be used any number of ways: to stuff potatoes or to serve over hot noodles or steamed vegetables and rice. During the summer months herbs are plentiful. This is a grand way to use fresh herbs to make a quick sauce that can be used for many family favorites.

1. Place all of the ingredients in a blender or food processor and blend until smooth. Start off with the least amount of vegetable broth and add more if needed to ensure a smooth consistency.

Caramel Sauce

ONE DAY I WANTED something caramel-y on my coconut milk ice cream, and I came up with this recipe. When you are cooking this sauce, be sure you don't let it cook so long that it turns into crystal—you want to be able to get it out of the jar. You can keep this around for months, and it is still good. You may have to heat it up in a pan with water in the bottom to soften it, but it doesn't go bad, so that's the good news!

1. Place the sorghum syrup, maple syrup, and agave in a saucepan and heat over medium-high heat. Heat to boiling and then add in the margarine and stir until it melts. Bring the mixture back to a boil and then add in the arrowroot powder. Whisk the mixture really well, so the arrowroot is well incorporated.

2. When the mixture is at a full rolling boil, reduce the heat to medium and cook for about 15 to 20 minutes, or until the mixture begins to caramelize.

3. Turn off the heat and stir in the vanilla, mixing it well. Pour the sauce into a jar and set on the counter to cool completely. Store in the refrigerator until ready to use.

MAKES ABOUT 1 PINT

⅓ cup sorghum syrup
2 tablespoons organic maple syrup
⅓ cup agave nectar
½ cup vegan margarine
2 tablespoons arrowroot powder
¼ teaspoon vanilla

Cashew Butter or
Peanut Butter Frosting

MAKES ABOUT 2 CUPS

3 tablespoons vegan buttery
    spread (soy-free spread is
    my preference)
1 cup unsalted cashew butter
    (or creamy peanut butter)
⅔ cup organic powdered
    sugar
1 teaspoon vanilla
Coconut milk (or other
    nondairy milk) as needed
    for consistency

I LOVE CASHEWS, so my preference is to use cashew butter in this recipe, but it tastes very good made with peanut butter too. Macadamia nut butter would also be nice and creamy. This frosting is especially good on the Chocolate Cupcakes (page 77). If you use cashew butter, be sure it is unsalted.

1. Combine the buttery spread and cashew butter in a small bowl, and using a hand mixer, beat until smooth. Slowly add the powdered sugar, a little at a time, beating on medium speed until you incorporate all of the sugar. Add the vanilla. If you need to add some milk to the mixture so it is spreadable, do so at this time.

Fresh Berry Compote

ONE DOLLOP PACKS a wallop! Try this on pancakes, ice cream, or over your favorite fruit. I like using fresh blueberries, strawberries, and raspberries out of the garden, but any combination will do.

MAKES ABOUT 2 CUPS

2 tablespoons vegan margarine
1 to 1½ cups fresh berries
3 tablespoons maple syrup (or agave nectar or sugar)
½ cup orange juice
½ to 1 tablespoon arrowroot

1. Heat the margarine in a medium skillet until melted. Add the berries, maple syrup, and orange juice. Heat to boiling.

2. Add the arrowroot, stir to thicken, and reduce heat to simmer. Continue stirring until desired consistency is achieved.

Maple-Pumpkin Butter

MAKES ABOUT 3 PINTS

3 cups organic canned
    pumpkin
Juice of 1 orange,
    approximately ½ cup
Seeds from ½ vanilla bean
    (or ½ teaspoon vanilla
    extract)
½ teaspoon freshly grated
    nutmeg
½ teaspoon cinnamon
½ teaspoon cardamom
1½ cups organic maple syrup

THIS WILL MAKE your house smell SO amazing when it is in the oven! You can use this butter on pumpkin waffles, as a filling in sweet potato biscuits, or as a yummy spread on your favorite gluten-free bread. A jar of Maple Pumpkin Butter also makes a thoughtful and delicious gift! This recipe takes approximately one hour to prepare.

1. Preheat oven to 350ºF. In a large bowl, combine all ingredients, mixing well. Transfer to a 9 x 9-inch baking dish. Bake until thickened, stirring regularly to ensure even cooking.

Orange Icing

IF YOU WANT something to give your muffins or cake some zing, consider an icing. This icing can be used for tea breads, cupcakes (such as the Pumpkin Cupcakes on page 83 or the Chocolate Cupcakes on page 77), or for cakes. Icings are different from frostings in that they are not meant to be slathered on a cake or muffin, but rather are meant to be drizzled. And if you like your icing thick, by all means, add some powdered sugar to this and it will thicken.

1. In a small bowl, whisk together all of the icing ingredients until well blended and smooth. Drizzle over the top of the muffins or whatever else you wish!

MAKES ABOUT ¹/₂ CUP

¼ cup Earth Balance or other vegan margarine

¼ teaspoon vanilla

2 tablespoons orange juice (fresh squeezed, if possible)

1½ cups powdered sugar

Creamy Cashew Milk

MAKES 1 QUART

1 cup raw organic cashews
4 cups water
1 to 2 teaspoons maple
   syrup (optional)
Vanilla extract

GOT CASHEW MILK? Cholesterol-free and high in B vitamins, copper, and magnesium, this milk is an excellent alternative to soy. Try a spot in your coffee or tea, over a bowl of your favorite cereal, or in a milkshake or smoothie. Personally, I like mine straight up and ice cold!

1. Place the cashews in a bowl, cover with water and soak overnight.

2. Pour the nuts and water into a blender and liquefy for 1 to 2 minutes until white and frothy.

3. Strain the mixture through a cheesecloth, using a wooden spoon or spatula to gently press the cashew mixture through the cloth. Though cashews don't have visible skins like almonds, you will end up with approximately ¼ cup pulp remaining. Add maple syrup and vanilla to taste.

Detox Drink

WHAT'S BETTER THAN drinking something that not only tastes good, but is good for you? Instead of reaching for that second cup of coffee, I recommend that you give this juice a try! You will need an electric juicer for this recipe—a blender or food processor will not suffice. Be sure to use organic fruits and vegetables.

1. Depending on the type of juicer you have, you will need to chop your vegetables and fruit to the appropriate size. I run the kale through my juicer first, followed by the carrots, parsley, then the celery, apple, and beet. Add in the lemon juice and cinnamon before serving. If you wish, you can add ice, but I drink it just as it is.

SERVES 2

1 cup kale, de-stemmed

5 medium carrots, ends removed

½ cup fresh parsley

½ cup celery, ends trimmed

1 large tart apple (Gala, Fiji, etc.), cored and quartered

1 red or yellow beet, peeled, ends trimmed, and cut to size to fit into a juicer

1 tablespoon lemon juice (fresh squeezed, please)

½ teaspoon cinnamon

acknowledgments

I would like to thank everyone who supported me during the development of this cookbook. I was fortunate to have many taste testers and recipe testers and much typing assistance and expert editing support. Special thanks to Katie McHugh at Perseus Books, who welcomed the idea of a sequel to *The Gluten-Free Vegan*, and to Lori Hobkirk at the Book Factory for managing the project.

I apologize if I have forgotten to mention anyone who tasted or tested recipes or supported me during the writing of this cookbook. I would like to acknowledge the following:

Carol Dudley, Stephanie Ann, Dara Morgan, Tammy Mills, the entire staff at Whole Foods Market in Gig Harbor, Alby Allen, Mike Carver, Lorraine Gill, Sarah and Jack from Metropolitan Market in Tacoma, Connie Harrington, Larry Miller, Walter Heilig and family, Jeff and Carrie Cheek and family, Nolan Kuzmick and family, Kevin and Lori Gray and family, Ben and Sue Berger and family, Karen and John McDonnell, Karen Wilkerson, Marcia Doran, Donna Daily, Elizabeth Bloom, Sally Priest, Sheila Quinn, Barb Schiltz, Dan Lukaczer, Rory Berthiaume, Jessie Bjorklund, Jeff Fors, Nathan Fors, Kimberly Napier, Liz Merrit, Zack Rosenbloom, Sally Johnson, Keith Yoshida, Terry O'Brien, Susan Hostetler, Kate Kenny, Alan Searle, Nicole Searle, Barbara Allen, Myles Ambrose, Kristine Darling, Thiago Garcia, Gay and Ken McCray, Beth Christ, Mary Adams, Gordy Rawson, Peter Somoff, the staff at the Institute for Functional Medicine in Gig Harbor, Sherrie Brewer,

Steve Hale, Brent Holbrook, Michael Stone, The Gig Harbor Gluten Free Group members, Amy Smith, Sharon Williams, Debbie and Eldon Friesen, Terry O'Grady, Jennifer Yellowless and family, Daniel Roso and family.

Special thanks to Keith Yoshida for developing my new website, www.susanobrien.org, helping me with everything techno and assisting me with the photo shoot. You are amazing and I am very grateful for all of your help!!

To Barb Schiltz, who edited the book prior to submission to Perseus. Your contributions were a huge help, and I am grateful for your gifts of time, expertise, and honest feedback. Thank you!

To Kristine Darling, whose work as a recipe tester went beyond my greatest hopes. Thank you for all of your efforts and extremely detailed recommendations! Thank you and Thiago for also being recipe tasters!

Thank you to my son Rory for helping me type up the recipes. I greatly appreciated your help.

Special thanks to my family, especially to Rory; Jeff; my daughter-in-law, Jessie; and my amazing grandson, Nathan. Thank you also to my dad, who cheered me on throughout the writing of the book!

APPENDIX I:
cooking equivalents

COOKING EQUIVALENTS

A pinch or dash		will be slightly less than ⅛ teaspoon
3 tsp	=	1 tablespoon
4 tbs	=	¼ cup
2 tbs	=	1 liquid oz.
1 cup	=	½ pint
4 cups of flour	=	1 pound flour
2 cups of liquid	=	16 oz
1 cup uncooked rice	=	2 cups cooked rice
1 lemon	=	¼ cup lemon juice
1 tsp. chia seeds mixed	=	1 egg (replacement) with 2 tbs. water

METRIC CONVERSIONS

✓ The recipes in this book have not been tested with metric measurements, so some variations might occur. Remember that the weight of dry ingredients varies according to the volume or density factor: 1 cup of flour weighs far less than 1 cup of sugar, and 1 tablespoon doesn't necessarily hold 3 teaspoons.

GENERAL FORMULA FOR METRIC CONVERSION

Ounces to grams	multiply ounces by 28.35
Grams to ounces	multiply ounces by 0.035
Pounds to grams	multiply pounds by 453.5
Pounds to kilograms	multiply pounds by 0.45
Cups to liters	multiply cups by 0.24
Fahrenheit to Celsius	subtract 32 from Fahrenheit temperature, multiply by 5, divide by 9
Celsius to Fahrenheit	multiply Celsius temperature by 9, divide by 5, add 32

OVEN TEMPERATURE EQUIVALENTS

FAHRENHEIT (F) AND CELSIUS (C)

100°F	=	38°C
200°F	=	95°C
250°F	=	120°C
300°F	=	150°C
350°F	=	180°C
400°F	=	205°C
450°F	=	230° C

LINEAR MEASUREMENTS

½ in	=	1½ cm
1 inch	=	2½ cm
6 inches	=	15 cm
8 inches	=	20 cm
10 inches	=	25 cm
12 inches	=	30 cm
20 inches	=	50 cm

WEIGHT (MASS) MEASUREMENTS

1 ounce	=	30 grams		
2 ounces	=	55 grams		
3 ounces	=	85 grams		
4 ounces	=	¼ pound	=	125 grams
8 ounces	=	½ pound	=	240 grams
12 ounces	=	¾ pound	=	375 grams
16 ounces	=	1 pound	=	454 grams

VOLUME (DRY) MEASUREMENTS

¼ teaspoon	=	1 milliliter
½ teaspoon	=	2 milliliters
¾ teaspoon	=	4 milliliters
1 teaspoon	=	5 milliliters
1 tablespoon	=	15 milliliters
¼ cup	=	59 milliliters
⅓ cup	=	79 milliliters
½ cup	=	118 milliliters
⅔ cup	=	158 milliliters
¾ cup	=	177 milliliters
1 cup	=	225 milliliters
4 cups or 1 quart	=	1 liter
½ gallon	=	2 liters
1 gallon	=	4 liters

VOLUME (LIQUID) MEASUREMENTS

1 teaspoon	=	⅙ fluid ounce	=	5 milliliters
1 tablespoon	=	½ fluid ounce	=	15 milliliters
2 tablespoons	=	1 fluid ounce	=	30 milliliters
¼ cup	=	2 fluid ounces	=	60 milliliters
⅓ cup	=	2⅔ fluid ounces	=	79 milliliters
½ cup	=	4 fluid ounces	=	118 milliliters
1 cup or ½ pint	=	8 fluid ounces	=	250 milliliters
2 cups or 1 pint	=	16 fluid ounces	=	500 milliliters
4 cups or 1 quart	=	32 fluid ounces	=	1,000 milliliters
1 gallon	=	4 liters		

Amy's. Amy provides gluten-free meals and also vegan meals. The only drawback to her products is that they may be made on equipment used for gluten products. She has several gluten-free meals. Many of her gluten-free products do include dairy. http://www.amyskitchen.com

Bob's Red Mill. Flours, mixes, etc. http://www.bobsredmill.com

Celiac Sprue Association. National celiac support group that provides tons of helpful information. http://www.csaceliacs.info

Celiac Disease Foundation. Provides support, information, and lots of great information. http://www.celiac.org

Follow Your Heart cheese alternatives: http://www.followyourheart.com

Gluten Free Mall. They have a plethora of information and resources available, such as foods, books, cleaning products, and much, much more. http://www.celica.com

National Foundation for Celiac Awareness is a nonprofit organization that is involved in gluten-free research. Its website provides a wealth of information about celiac disease as well as well as updated blogs and links to helpful information. http://www.celiaccentral.org

Living Without. A great magazine with wonderful recipes and stories about living gluten-free. http://www.livingwithout.com

Gluten-Free Living. This magazine and its website provide gluten-free support with tons of helpful resources. http://www.glutenfreeliving.com

GFCFDiet.com This site offers dietary support for individuals with autism. They provide resources, Q&A, shopping guides, etc. http://www.gfcfdiet.com

Ener-G.com. This site has tons of gluten-free products, but they are best known for their egg replacer. I use it in many of the recipes in my cookbooks. http://www.ener-g.com

Lundberg Family Farms sells brown rice syrup, rice noodles, and other rice products. http://www.lundberg.com

Galaxy Foods has tons of soy-free, dairy-free cheese options to choose from. http://www.galaxyfoods.com

Enjoy Life Foods. This company is great. Their products are gluten-free, soy-free, dairy-free, nut-free, egg-free, GMO-free, and kosher. They have several items on the market shelves. www.http://enjoylifefoods.com

WayFare Foods provides nondairy, non-soy cheese alternatives. http://www.wayfarefoods.com

Coconut Bliss makes Coconut Bliss ice cream. It is heavenly and comes in several flavors. I love it, and I bet you will too! http://coconutbliss.com

So Delicious is my favorite drinking milk, and I love their other products as well. They make a nondairy creamer, ice cream, and yogurt too. They can be found at http://www.sodeliciousdairyfree.com

Triumph Dining. A wonderful site that provides restaurant guides, grocery guides, and a blog for updates. http://www.triumphdining.com

VegFamily is a magazine that provides great information for the entire family. *VegFamily* offers information on vegan recipes, foods, chocolate, clothing, gifts, and much more. The website is very comprehensive and provides lots of information and a discussion forum as well. http://www.vegfamily.com

Vegan Essentials is a company that provides everything you want to know about where to shop for vegan essentials. The company provides some foods, but not all of the products they sell are gluten-free. http://www.veganessentials.com

Eco-Vegan Gal has tons of great information on her website. She features vegan products on her website and also many gluten-free ones as well. She can be found at http://www.ecovegangal.com.

index